ALSO BY MATTHEW KELLY

The Rhythm of Life

The Seven Levels of Intimacy

The Dream Manager

Building Better Families

Perfectly Yourself

PERFECTLY YOURSELF

9 Lessons for
Enduring Happiness

MATTHEW KELLY

BALLANTINE BOOKS

New York

2008 Ballantine Books Trade Paperback Edition

Copyright © 2006 by Beacon Publishing

Published in the United States by Ballantine Books, an imprint of
The Random House Publishing Group, a division of Random House, Inc., New York.

BALLANTINE and colophon are registered trademarks
of Random House, Inc.

Originally published in hardcover in the United States by Ballantine Books, an imprint
of The Random House Publishing Group, a division of Random House, Inc., in 2006.

Library of Congress Cataloging-in-Publication Data

Kelly, Matthew.
Perfectly yourself : 9 lessons for enduring happiness / by Matthew Kelly.
    p.   cm.
ISBN 978-0-345-49452-8
1. Self-realization.   I. Title.

BJ1470.K45 2006
158.1—dc22   2006043024

Printed in the United States of America

www.ballantinebooks.com

6 8 9 7 5

Book design by Mary A. Wirth

Contents

$\mathcal{F}$or decades we have been told that we live in a consumer society. At this point I doubt many would argue with the assertion, but I do have some questions. Are we still the consumers, or are we being consumed? Have we lost something of ourselves to this unbridled consumerism? Can we get it back?

I look around, and it seems everything has a brand on it these days. The proliferation of brands has blanketed our society and has powerfully impacted our psyche. Again I have some questions. What did we first use branding on? Cattle. What did the branding signify? Ownership. What was our second use of branding? Slavery. And that branding signified what? Ownership. Do we own the brands or do the brands own us? Are we still the consumers, or are we being consumed?

Though we take pride in our individualism and independence, we seem particularly enamored of fitting in. To a certain extent, the desire to fit in and be accepted is natural and normal. But when it comes at the cost of losing sight of who we are as marvelously unique individuals, something is amiss.

Let us seek to discover once more what it means to be perfectly ourselves.

PERFECTLY YOURSELF

One

Are You Making Progress?

Our differences as individuals are fascinating and wonderful, and this book is about exploring and celebrating what makes us unique. But I want to begin by identifying what drives our desire to become perfectly ourselves. In my work with more than three million people over the past decade, I have often stood in awe of how wonderfully unique we are as individuals, but I have also been intrigued by the astonishing similarities that exist between men and women of all ages and cultures, all countries and creeds. The greatest of these similarities is what I like to call "the hunger": a common yearning in people's hearts for something more or for something that has been lost, a yearning that seems to be growing stronger and deeper with every passing day.

Some people associate this hunger with a desire for more money or more sex. Others respond to this hunger by seeking the perfect partner, thinking that this one person will calm the yearning once and for all. Others collect possessions or amass power in an attempt to quell the hunger. But it seems unquenchable, insatiable. There are some who associate the hunger with a need for more fulfillment in the workplace. Others sense that something is wrong but cannot quite put their finger on it, so they take journeys hoping to discover something about themselves.

Sooner or later this hunger tends to lead most people to the area of personal development. Some people turn their attention to health and well-being, others to gaining financial independence, others to improving a relationship, and some to spirituality.

The hunger is really a desire to be more perfectly yourself. It can express itself in hundreds of ways, but all are born from the single desire to feel more at home with who you are. Regardless of what area of personal development you choose to focus on at this time in your life, there are certain stages and pitfalls that are common to all. They all share a common psychology of change. This book is about understanding the dynamics of change, the change that we desire but that so often eludes us.

Trying to lose weight is a perfect example.

Every January, a slew of new diet books are published. Many people have gained weight over the holidays, and publishers know we will resolve at New Year's to slim down. One of these books will break out and hit the top of all the best-seller lists. Everyone will be talking about it. The diet will be presented as miraculous. People will flock to the book. Everybody will rave about it as if simply reading the book will cause weight to fall from bodies as effortlessly as beads of sweat.

The thing is, you and I both know that twelve months ago they were talking about another book in the same way. And next year, there will be more new and amazing diet books. Editors in all the Manhattan publishing houses are sitting at their desks right now trying to figure out what will be the next big diet book.

People seem obsessed with losing weight, and yet Americans

are becoming more and more obese with every passing year. Is it just me, or is there a massive disconnect here?

This book is about that disconnect. Regardless of what area of your life you would like to transform, I want to show you how we bridge the gap between our *desire for change* and actually *creating real and sustainable change* in our lives.

A MOMENT OF TRUTH

From time to time my friend Meggie will get this look on her face, and I know exactly what she is about to say: "Matthew, get honest with yourself!" I love that about her. She doesn't say it that often, so when she does it means something.

I think we all need moments of honesty from time to time. We need them as individuals, as couples, as families, and as nations. In the area of personal development, we are in desperate need of a moment of truth. We need to get honest with ourselves.

The truth is this: Diets don't fail. We fail at diets. Savings plans don't fail. We fail at savings plans. Exercise routines don't fail. We fail at exercise routines. Relationships don't fail. We fail at relationships.

This may seem harsh, but until we face this difficult truth, we will never seriously ask the really important questions that loom in the back of our minds: *Why do I fail every time I go on a diet? Why can't I stick to my budget and savings plan? Why can't I be consistent about working out? Why am I constantly in and out of relationships?* And so on.

Once we start asking these tough questions, we discover another fundamental truth about the whole process of change. People don't fail because they want to fail. People don't go on diets to gain weight. People don't get married to get divorced. People don't join a gym and sign a two-year contract to drop out three months later.

Whether we are dealing with the area of health and well-being, relationships, finances, career, or spirituality, people want to advance. We have an enormous desire to grow and change and improve ourselves. *So why don't we?* I hear you ask. *What's the problem? Why is it that so many of us seem unable to transform resolutions into habits?*

This book is about learning a new way.

The reason most of us fail to achieve real and sustainable change in our lives is because we focus too much on the desired outcome and not enough on the progress we are making. It is important to establish goals, but they can often seem overwhelming and impossible. If we can condition ourselves to focus on the progress we are making, our advances will encourage us to persevere in achieving our goals and dreams. It is when we lose sight of our progress that we become discouraged, and it is discouragement that often lands us back in our old self-defeating habits and self-destructive behaviors.

JUST BE YOURSELF

Before the beginning of time, when you were just a dream, your purpose had already been assigned. Purposefully created, and created for a purpose, you are here at this very moment to become the-best-version-of-yourself—not to become some poor imitation of your parents, your friends, your siblings, or your colleagues— but to become perfectly yourself.

Life is not about doing and having; it is about becoming.

Could you have a better dream for your children than to want them to become the-best-version-of-themselves? Could you have a better dream for your spouse than to want him or her to become the-best-version-of-him- or herself? It is the ultimate dream—and when we turn our attention to living this dream, our lives are flooded with energy, enthusiasm, passion, purpose, and a real and sustainable joy. It is time to start living the dream.

When we are healthy in a holistic sense, or in any one aspect of our lives, we are driven by this dream to become the-best-version-of-ourselves. Why are there so many products and programs available that help people transform different areas of their lives? Because there is an enormous demand for them. Marketers know that people have this insatiable desire to improve themselves. This desire is what drives us when we are healthiest.

When we are unhealthy, we tend to abandon our true selves, often wishing we were more like someone else or that we were someone else altogether. This is often most noticeable during adolescence, when people grapple with identity issues. But many of us develop a permanent contempt for ourselves (or for certain aspects of ourselves) during this period of development. This contempt for self stifles our dreams.

Living the dream and striving to become all we are capable of being is the only thing you ever truly need to answer for, and our only regrets come from abandoning our true selves. Are you celebrating your true self, or are you still trying to be the person you think other people want you to be—or the person you think other people will like?

Now is your time. There will never be a better time to begin. It is time now to peel back the layers of conditioning and expectations that have encrusted your heart and mind. It is time to become perfectly yourself.

The first step toward becoming perfectly yourself is acknowledging your imperfections. It may seem ironic, or even paradoxical, but life is often like that. Making peace with your imperfections is as much a part of being perfectly yourself as striving to improve the aspects of your character that have become distorted by experience or habit. It is essential for health of mind, body, and spirit that we recognize that what we often consider to be our imperfections are actually part of our perfection.

The challenge is to discern which of your imperfections are part of who you are when you are perfectly yourself and which are a distortion of your true self. A fine and often hazy line separates these two realities.

A woman with a bubbly personality should not abandon it simply because some people don't like it. It is part of her best and truest self.

You may not be a details person. It's not necessarily a defect. It may just be part of who you are. Everyone doesn't have to be a details person. It doesn't give you permission to be negligent about your commitments, and to some extent you can improve your ability to manage details, but you shouldn't take a job that requires you to constantly manage details, and it would be wise to surround yourself with people who thrive on taking care of the details.

Similarly, your daughter may not excel in math. Her brain may simply be wired to excel in other areas. It is entirely possible that her best self is a poor mathematician. A certain level of practical knowledge in this area is necessary, but she need not be forced to master the upper reaches of mathematics.

On the other hand, if a man is rude and impatient, it is not because these are an expression of his best self; it is rather that they are an expression of behaviors that have been practiced. Personality tendencies and talents should be accepted, but character defects should always be challenged.

Consciously, subconsciously, semiconsciously, we are all preoccupied with this attempt to be more perfectly who we really are at the essence of our being. But think of it in this way: A tree does not try to make all of its branches straight. It is perfect in its imperfection, perfectly imperfect. And yet it does change and grow over time.

The answer, for you and me, is to *try* to live in that delicate balance between striving to improve in character while celebrating our unique personality and talents. Lean too much to one side, and you will smother your wonderful and unique personality. Tend too much to the other, and you will abandon the character that is the source of dignity and self-respect.

We cannot rush to achieve this delicate balance. Often, as soon as it is found, it is lost, and we find ourselves searching for it again. But as we look back on any day or week, there are moments when we can honestly and humbly say, "For that moment I was the-best-version-of-myself!" We need to learn to recognize those moments, understand their secrets, celebrate them, and duplicate them. These moments will help us to find the balance between acceptance of self and our need for change. We must approach this place of balance between accepting ourselves for who we are and challenging ourselves to be all we are capable of being like one would approach a high-spirited animal—calmly and slowly.

I had a friend and mentor once who used to say two things to me repeatedly: "Be kind to yourself" and "All great things can only be achieved with a light heart." This great soul is lost from my life now, but his words endure. Kindness toward ourselves precedes all genuine and lasting growth, and lightheartedness is a sign that we trust that we are exactly where we are right now for a reason.

Better, Not Best

This idea of being gentle with ourselves and the role of progress collided powerfully for me last summer after a friend shared an insight about one of the central premises of my teaching. Rick and I had become friends when he and his wife attended one of my seminars in Italy a few years back. He has a wonderful sense of humor and is filled with a wonderful curiosity and a healthy skepticism, and I find his company invigorating.

Last summer he and his son were sitting around with me before one of my seminars. We were goofing around a bit, and his son was doing uncanny impressions of anyone we would name. We were catching up, and he was telling me about his work in China and how much that country has changed in the last ten years. Our conversation then turned to my work, and he said something that touched me deeply and got me thinking. In one sentence, he was able to articulate something that I have always felt from certain people in the audience but have never been quite able to articulate or even put my finger on: "Matthew, I think your idea about becoming the-best-version-of-yourself is fantastic. It clarifies so many things in our everyday lives, from the little decisions to the big life-changing choices, but some people just can't get their minds around the notion of the-best-version-of-themselves. They need you simply to speak to them about a-better-version-of-themselves."

I saw it instantly.

For more than a decade, I had been speaking to people about becoming the-best-version-of-themselves, giving them examples of how to improve physically, emotionally, intellectually, and spiritually. Audiences have always responded very well to the message. They have been inspired by the idea. But now it dawned on me that for some people the idea of becoming the-best-version-of-themselves was just too daunting. I had to break it down into manageable portions.

People are always asking me questions such as "When will I know that I have become the-best-version-of-myself?" and "Do I ever become the-best-version-of-myself, or is it one of those things we strive for but never achieve?"

Well, it isn't like we wake up one day and say, "The job is done.

I am the-best-version-of-myself!" Every day we have to celebrate our best self. In every moment, we choose between the-best-version-of-ourselves and myriad second-rate-versions-of-ourselves.

In some moments, we actively celebrate our best self and know that we are indeed the-best-version-of-ourselves. But in the next moment we can lose our best self once again to laziness, impatience, anger, envy, gossip, greed, thoughtlessness, selfishness . . .

The-best-version-of-ourselves isn't something we strive for and never achieve. It is something we achieve in some moments and not in others.

Your essential purpose is to become the-best-version-of-yourself. This one principle brings clarity to everything else in our lives. What makes a book, friend, marriage, job, or movie good? It is that it helps us to become the-best-version-of-ourselves! Everything makes sense in relation to our essential purpose. The people, experiences, and things we fill our lives with either help us to become the-best-version-of-ourselves or they don't. In every moment we simply need to ask ourselves, "Which of the options before me will help me to become the-best-version-of-myself?"

We need to be aware of the goal, no doubt. Let's face it, it is only progress if you are moving in the right direction. But the journey that leads to our essential purpose needs to be broken up into practical and manageable stages.

Reflecting on Rick's words that day, I began to break down the journey of becoming the-best-version-of-ourselves. Then I began to examine the psychology of change by asking questions such as "What takes place in our minds as we begin to implement change in our lives?"

I began with a self-examination.

When I was very young, about six years old, as I recall, I was sent off once a week for piano lessons. My mother had decided that all her sons would play the piano. I hated piano lessons and would complain every week. That was my first encounter with the maxim, "Practice makes perfect." My piano teacher would say it over and over again. My parents would reinforce the teacher's message by telling me the same thing.

I now know that practice doesn't make perfect. Practice makes progress. And practice makes progress only if you practice the right things in the right way.

Piano lessons lasted only six months before my mother allowed me to quit. A couple of other times I was enrolled in classes, but they too were short-lived. It was not until I was about seventeen that I started playing the piano. I remember going to a party one night, and a friend of mine sat down at a piano and started playing, and everyone else started singing along. I had never heard anyone play popular music on the piano. I decided that night that I was going to learn to play the piano. Not my teacher's way, not my parents' way, but my way.

The next day I sat down at the piano at home and started feeling my way around the keys. At first it was painful and tedious, but over time and with practice, I developed a sense for how music moved and flowed, and a style that allowed me to learn tunes relatively quickly, though certainly not perfectly.

Today I love to play the piano. I don't play anything perfectly from a technical point of view, but to me that doesn't matter. With every passing year, I get better on the piano, but the main thing is that I love playing. The piano has become a great therapy, a way to relax and unwind from the pressures of daily living.

In many things, *perfect* is much more subjective than many people would have you believe and much less objective than we would often allow ourselves to believe. A perfect relationship for you may be very different from a perfect relationship for me. Some people are enamored of whatever type of generic beauty is plastered on the covers of magazines, but I am more attracted to people who are comfortable in their body. Perfection has many expressions.

How many different ways are there to pursue perfection? At this particular time in history, about six billion—one for every person on the face of the earth.

WHAT'S YOUR THING?

Some people struggle to keep to their budget. Other people struggle with their weight. Some struggle with a relationship. For other people, shopping and credit card debt is a problem. Some struggle with more destructive addictions. We all have something we struggle with, something that is holding us back. My thing is food.

I like food. It is no secret that I love chocolate, but my love affair with food doesn't stop there.

Name a city anywhere in the world, and there is a pretty good chance I can tell you what the best chocolate native to that city is and where to eat in that city, from fine dining to hole-in-the-wall haunts with greasy hamburgers. My mother makes the best meat loaf in the Southern Hemisphere, and Sue Robinson cooks the best meal in Cincinnati. Depending on where you are and what you are looking for, I can probably help you.

In New York there are lots of famous restaurants, but my personal favorite is Abboccato on 55th Street. If you are visiting Sydney, I would tell you not to leave without spending a day at Manly Beach and having lunch at the Blue Water Cafe. Mama Zoe's is a completely candlelit Cajun restaurant in Dublin. It is an unlikely location, but the food is amazing nonetheless. And if it's chocolate you like, then I can tell you the best American-made chocolates are the milk chocolate coconut clusters and raisin clusters from Betsy Ann Chocolates in Pittsburgh. Other than that, See's Candies makes a great Scotchmallow that's worth a taste if you find yourself on the West Coast. In Sydney, Haigh's at the Strand Arcade is going to be your sort of place. If you are looking for hot chocolate, Angelina's in Paris or the café in the main square of Assisi, Italy, is where you want to be.

Yes, food is definitely my thing.

I eat when I am happy. I eat when I am sad. I eat to celebrate. I eat to comfort myself. I eat to reward myself. I eat when I am writing. I eat when I get writer's block. I eat.

All of this eating creates a bit of a problem. I start to gain weight.

So then I go on a diet or an exercise kick. I eat good food and exercise like a maniac for a couple of weeks, and I am feeling great. Then I get on the scales and I have lost only two pounds. In many ways this is great. The problem is that I want to lose twenty pounds. So I get depressed that I have lost "only" two and begin to focus on the eighteen I haven't lost.

Sound familiar?

Rather than celebrating the two that I have lost, I allow the other eighteen to depress me. I don't celebrate my progress; I focus on my lack of perfection.

The next day I get tempted to abandon my diet in some small way or become a little lazy in my self-prescribed exercise regimen, and this small deviation becomes the crack in the dam. Self-pity begins to sink in, and I begin to overindulge myself again. Then I get even more down on myself because I wasn't able to keep the rules I set for myself.

For a few weeks I ignore the problem, but then I begin to feel lethargic and I miss the vitality I was feeling for the brief period when I was eating well and exercising regularly. I tell myself that if I could maintain that healthy lifestyle, I could do extraordinary things and write amazing books. So I decide to give it another go . . .

I make another whole set of rules for myself. The list goes

something like this: I can eat this and this every day; I can eat this and that only once a week. I'll exercise for forty-five minutes six times a week, and if I miss my exercise, I can't eat anything unhealthy on that day.

Yes, welcome to the madness of my mind.

For a couple of weeks this goes fine and I feel great. Then something will happen to upset me or I will just have a particularly tough day on the road, and I will turn to food for comfort and the whole plan will go out the window.

The cycle repeats itself a few more times, and before I know it, I have a pattern of defeat.

PATTERNS OF DEFEAT

Patterns of defeat come to define our lives. We want to change, we have tried to change, but we have failed so many times and start to think that we can't change. This is a huge blow to our self-esteem, which means that a pattern of defeat usually signifies the beginning of some form of self-loathing.

We stop thinking about the-best-version-of-ourselves now and avoid anything that reminds us of it. We drown our sadness in music or television or anything that can distract us from what is really happening inside us.

We are hesitant to make New Year's resolutions because we doubt we have the strength of will to honor them. We start to think and read more about other people's lives as a way of escaping from our own. We drink more, eat more, sleep more, shop more, and seek more of every pleasure that can distract us from what is really going on within us. The discouragement of defeat leads us to the place where we don't want to be ourselves at all—let alone the-best-version-of-ourselves.

While all of this is going on, we have the sense that something is wrong and is whispering to us from within, but we ignore that voice.

Paralyzed by the fear of failing again, we are afraid to hope. We are scared of subscribing to false hope. So we begin to despise anything to do with personal development and perhaps anyone committed to it. They represent a dream that has been lost or abandoned, though we don't know which. At this moment of disillusionment and disgust, we become filled with profound questions about ourselves, but we avoid them. Inwardly we are overwhelmed with all manner of self-doubt, but externally we may pump up the signs of our confidence to compensate.

We wonder to ourselves: *Why am I unable to change? Is it my fault, or is this just who I am?*

The answer, of course, is both.

All of this goes on until we become so desperate that we are all but forced to change. The doctor tells you that if you don't lay off the fried foods, you will die of a heart attack, or that if you don't stop smoking, you will have to have a lung removed. Perhaps your wife tells you that if you don't spend more time with your family, she is going to leave you. For many it is an increasing dependence on drugs or alcohol that overwhelms and debilitates them, bringing them to their knees in desperation.

These are the lucky ones in many ways. It is sad how they had to come to it. But many alcoholics will tell you that their lives didn't begin until they hit rock bottom. They will also tell you horrific stories from before they stopped drinking.

Why are the people who come to radical forks in the road the lucky ones? Because most people never get to that point of desperation and so never change. It's said that an alcoholic must choose to live a spiritual life or to die an alcoholic death. There is nothing in between for an alcoholic. If a change in diet becomes a life-and-death situation, most people become quickly motivated and re-solved. Most people change only when the pain of not changing becomes greater than the pain required to change.

But most people, perhaps you and I, can more likely muddle along in patterns of defeat and self-loathing without drawing much attention to ourselves. All of this can be going on inside us, and most people would be completely oblivious to it. The people around us can love us and feel loved by us. Little do they know how incapable of love we truly are because we are so filled with the kind of self-loathing that prevents us from loving anybody, including ourselves.

If someone does recognize our plight, it is probably because they have been in a similar situation. This person may try to reach out to us or challenge us, but now we take refuge behind the great excuse: "This is who I am!" As with most lies, if you tell it often enough, you will start to believe it. And as we grow more and more comfortable with the lie and less and less comfortable with our-selves, we begin to add emotional manipulation to situations like this by adding, "Why can't you just love me for who I am?"

We say, "This is who I am!" but secretly we despise who we have become and desperately want to become the self we know we are capable of being. But we feel trapped. And we are. We are trapped by our illusions of perfection, depressed by the difficulty of the road ahead, overwhelmed by our patterns of defeat.

What I have described here happens to many, many people. It is happening to millions of people as I write these words and will be happening to just as many more people as you read them.

People want to change. We know that there are certain areas of our lives that we would desperately like to transform. Be honest with yourself for a moment. What is the one thing about yourself that would most radically improve your life if you changed it?

Have you tried? Of course you have. Are you still trying, or have you given up?

Can people substantially change?

This question represents the abyss we all find ourselves teetering on at least once in our lives, and until we are convinced that substantial change is possible, our lives remain little more than a waking dream. The abyss is imagined; it is no more real than a child's nightmare. A new awareness of the power of progress can open our eyes so that we discover that what is before us is not an abyss but a path. The answer lies in taking the first step.

A pitcher doesn't throw a hundred-mile-per-hour fastball on his first attempt. First he learns to hold the ball, then he learns to throw the ball, and then he learns to throw the ball in the right direction. These steps are so fundamental that we overlook them. Only then does a pitcher begin to improve speed and accuracy. He throws a seventy-mile-per-hour ball before he throws an eighty-mile-per-hour ball, and a ninety-mile-per-hour ball before he throws that hundred-mile-per-hour fastball. There may be days when he can't throw as fast as he could the day before. In these moments, he must either celebrate his overall progress or focus on some aspect other than speed. He is not throwing as fast, but perhaps he is moving the ball better than he ever has or throwing with more accuracy. At every juncture, he celebrates his progress.

When a pitcher gets injured, he begins rehabilitation by going back to basics. He returns to the beginning, even to such fundamentals as learning to hold the ball again. A great rehab coach designs a plan with stages and goals along the way so that the recovering athlete can celebrate his progress.

Celebrating progress is fundamental in the psychology of change. In our culture we tend to celebrate by eating or buying things, but the celebration I speak of here is something that takes place within us. Celebrating progress means giving yourself a psychological pat on the back. There is nothing more powerful than the way you speak to yourself. Celebrating progress is the first secret to breaking those patterns of failure.

Another of the great secrets that we often overlook is that failure is a part of all great achievement and discovery.

We live in a culture obsessed with success, and as a result we unconsciously foster the attitude that it is not okay to fail. We often measure a person's value by his or her success. Of course, this judgment turns on us when we fail, and we tend to take it personally. If you fail, you aren't a failure.

I think baseball teaches us more about failure than any other sport does. A great hitter has a batting average of perhaps 350. What does that tell us? It tells us that he succeeds in hitting the ball only thirty-five percent of the time. What else does it tell us? It tells us that he fails sixty-five percent of the time.

Francis T. Vincent Jr., while commissioner of baseball, made these observations in a speech at Fairfield University:

> Baseball teaches us, or has taught most of us, how to deal with failure. We learn at a very young age that failure is the norm in baseball and, precisely because we have failed, we hold in high regard those who fail less often—those who hit safely in one out of three chances and become star players. I also find it fascinating that baseball, alone in sport, considers errors to be a part of the game, part of its rigorous truth.

We must never allow our spirit to be stifled by failure. Failure is a part of progress, not a final outcome.

Both Thomas Edison and Albert Einstein powerfully illustrated this lesson. Both of these men suffered through failure more than most, and yet they became our greatest inventor and mathematician, respectively. Day after day they grappled with trial and error, mistakes and frustration, disappointment and defeats, and moments of complete disillusionment. But they viewed these setbacks, adversities, defeats, and failures as clues to the discoveries they were seeking. They genuinely believed that their failures signified progress.

The story of Edison's effort to find a way to keep a lightbulb burning is well known. He tried more than ten thousand combinations of materials before he found the one that worked. People asked him later in his life how he could continue after failing that many times. He said he didn't see the other attempts as failures. He then went on to explain that he had successfully identified ten thousand ways that didn't work and that each attempt brought him closer to the one that would. He saw his failures as progress.

Einstein, whom many people believe to be the smartest man who ever lived, said, "I think and think for months and years. Ninety-nine times the conclusion is false. The hundredth time I am right."

Why do we perpetuate the belief that it is not okay to fail? Failure plays an important role in our development and a *critical* role in our attempts to become perfectly ourselves. Whatever pattern of defeat you may find yourself in right now, remember these three abiding truths:

1. Other people before you have successfully overcome the obstacles you face; seek them out and draw strength from their stories and example.
2. All of your past failures leave you better equipped than ever before to succeed in your next attempt.
3. It will never be easier to break that pattern of defeat than it is right now.

Allow the words of Benjamin Barber to echo deep within you:

I divide the world into learners and non-learners. There are
people who learn, who are open to what happens around them,
who listen, who hear the lessons. When they do something stu-
pid, they don't do it again. And when they do something that
works a little bit, they do it even better and harder the next time.
The question to ask is not whether you are a success or a failure,
but whether you are a learner or a non-learner.

THE POWER OF PROGRESS

Are you making progress? It's an important question to ask ourselves: "Am I making progress?" I have not had much experience
with being perfect, but I have had considerable experience with
making progress. The reason I point this out is because when I
am making progress, I am a happier person than when I am obsess-
ing about some idyllic vision of perfection that I am falling short
of. Progress animates us. It brings us to life. When we sense that we
are making progress, we tend to be filled with passion, energy, enthusiasm, purpose, and a real and sustainable joy. Progress fills us
with gratitude for the now and hope for the future. Progress creates enduring happiness.

So are you making progress? If you don't know, or if you have
to think about it too much, then you are probably not paying attention. That's the downfall of most people when it comes to the
area of personal development. We simply stop paying attention.
The other mistake we often make is to take it for granted that we
are making progress, as if adding another year to our lives is proof
of progress.

The only way you can answer the question of whether you are
making progress honestly and without hesitation is if you have

spent considerable time thinking about it before now. But it is a question whose answer evades most people. We can become so preoccupied with what we have and what we do that we lose sight of who we are and who we are becoming.

Are you making progress? Are you a better person today than you were a year ago? Are you happier? More fulfilled? Are you a better spouse? boyfriend? girlfriend? parent? child? employee? employer? teammate? colleague? citizen? friend? Are you healthier? Are you more financially independent than you were a year ago? Is your work becoming more and more satisfying? These are all important questions, but to answer them, we must first ask and answer this question: What is progress?

Shortly after World War II, Western culture became obsessed with progress. Make no mistake—every age has had its own obsession with progress. But what made the obsession with progress of the twentieth century different was that we quickly began to consider progress and change to be the same thing. In every aspect of society and culture, people began demanding change as if change was *always* a good thing and with the assumption that change *always* brought progress.

Western society has changed much in the past fifty years. Has the change always been for the better? Some would argue that it depends on what you consider *better*. But most reasonable people would concede that no, change has not always been for the better. During the past fifty years, for example, violence has escalated massively. It is a change, but most reasonable people would admit that it is not for the better.

Change doesn't equal progress. Change doesn't guarantee progress.

Progress is moving toward a goal. If your goal in the 1950s was to make our society more violent, then clearly you have achieved your goal. But most people, if asked in the 1950s "Would you like society to be more violent or less violent fifty years from now?" would have responded in favor of reduced violence. Violence has increased, so in this way we have not made progress. And worse than that, we have regressed as a society in this area.

Progress is change for the better. Progress is change that makes something more perfectly itself. Progress is any change, however small, that makes someone more perfectly himself or herself.

What, then, do we wish to progress toward? For every person, the answer would be different, and we will examine that shortly. But for a moment, let's ponder what collective preferences we have for progress.

Most reasonable people are of good will and hold very similar preferences when it comes to progress. They want the world to become a better place, and they want to live happier lives.

When we start to think about these preferences, they begin to transform into desires, and the more we think about them, the stronger the desires become, and the stronger the desires become, the more we align our actions with these desires and actually bring about the intended progress.

The problem is that most people spend very little time thinking about how they would like the world to become a better place, and so they make very little contribution when it comes to moving the world in that direction. If you asked them what their preference was, they would tell you that they would prefer the world to become a better place than to become a worse place. But their preference is never really transformed into desire and action.

Most people will tell you that they would prefer to live happier lives, but how much time do they actually spend thinking about how they could create and live a happier life? The preference never becomes desire. The desire never becomes action. But they will spend their whole lives preferring a happier life.

Preference is not enough. Progress requires desire and action.

It is not possible to create a genuinely happier life while not also making the world a better place. So let us progress in the direction of happier lives and a better world to pass on to our children and grandchildren.

No doubt, there will be some disagreement between different people about what constitutes "better" and "happier." We will explore this further a little later in the context of our discussion about the role character plays in our lives and society.

EVERY DAY IS YOUR FIRST SOMETHING

I recently spent a couple of days with friends in Atlanta who have a three-month-old daughter, their first child. My visit coincided with the Super Bowl, and I remarked that this would be Brooke's first Super Bowl. Her father, Nick, replied, "Every day is her first something."

In children, we celebrate progress. We applaud them, hug them, kiss them, congratulate them, and reward them for the tiniest advances. This atmosphere of encouragement plays a huge role in the rapid progress children make in the early months and years of their lives.

Just because we are adults, we shouldn't stop celebrating progress. Progress is a reward in itself. I am happier when I am making progress. See if the same isn't true for you. Observe yourself. Study the areas that you are making progress in. Look back at times in your life when you have made progress in an area of your life. How did you feel about yourself, about life, and about your future?

Our capacity for improvement is unfathomable. Whether it is professionally or personally, in the area of health and well-being, personal finances, relationships, diet and exercise, or character and spirituality, we have an extraordinary ability to improve. But to improve, we need to know ourselves very well. We need to be able to look beyond our obvious strengths and weaknesses and see our subtle tendencies. We need to be able to detect when we are lying to ourselves, when we could give more than we are giving, and when we are truly heading down the wrong path.

Over the years as I have studied many different forms and expressions of spirituality, I have been most surprised not by the differences between them but by their similarities. Of particular interest to us at this point is one practice that is found in all of the major expressions of spirituality, from Buddhism to Christianity, from Hinduism to Judaism. The practice has different names. Christians call it an examination of conscience, while Buddhists simply call it the daily examination. Regardless of what we call it, those who have taken personal development most seriously for thousands of years have employed this simple exercise not to measure perfection but to gauge progress.

Within every tradition there are a dozen different forms of this exercise, but in essence it comes down to taking a few moments at the end of each day to ask the question "Am I better today than I was yesterday?"

The answer to this question raises more questions: "What areas of my life do I need to improve?" "What areas of my life do I need to give more attention to?" "What behaviors are preventing me from making progress toward the-best-version-of-myself?"

Who you are today is only a shadow of who you are capable of being. It is our potential that most excites and frustrates us.

Baby steps are the secret. Small victories lead to large victories. The injured athlete has to take baby steps. During rehabilitation, trainers teach recovering superstars to celebrate small victories, just as a parent teaches a child to celebrate even the smallest advance. Let's start to pay attention to the question "Am I making progress?"

Are you making progress? As I said earlier, if you have to think about it, then you probably are not paying attention.

The first lesson for enduring happiness is this:

CELEBRATE YOUR PROGRESS.

Take time at the end of each day, even at intervals throughout the day, to reflect on the progress you have made. Consider the different areas of your life. In some, you will have made progress; celebrate that progress. In other areas, you may have stagnated or regressed; don't beat yourself up about it. Be gentle with yourself. You are a marvelous creation, but you are a work in progress.

Never end a period of examination without identifying some progress that you have made. As we move through the remaining chapters of this book and discover the other eight lessons for enduring happiness, you will discover many areas in which you can measure and celebrate progress.

To be perfectly ourselves is something we should all aspire to, but the path that leads us to the-best-version-of-ourselves is the path of progress. Let this be the inner dialogue that encourages us to progress a little more each day: "I am better today than I was yesterday."

Applying the First Lesson for
Enduring Happiness:

CELEBRATE YOUR PROGRESS

I will apply the first lesson of enduring happiness
to my life by taking the following steps:

1. I will focus my resolve by making one resolution at a time. When I make a resolution, I will define it in measurable and manageable terms, not lofty and immeasurable ideals. I will write my resolution down, along with a description of how my life will improve if I put this resolution into effect. Each day I will pause several times to review my resolution and the ways it will change me and my life. Once I have firmly established this resolution as a habit in my life, I will make my next resolution.

2. I will celebrate progress by giving myself a psychological pat on the back every time I make an effort in the direction of my resolution. I will rejoice in even the smallest victory, but at every major milestone I will celebrate the progress I have made in some special way. I will ritualize it in order to create a powerful memory. At times this celebration will be in solitude, and at other times I will invite others to celebrate with me. Remembering that how I talk to myself affects me more than how others talk to me, I will use my inner dialogue constantly throughout the day to encourage myself in becoming a-better-version-of-myself.

3. I will be mindful of first things and actively seek first things. From time to time I will consciously set out to do something for the first time, thus celebrating my infinite capacity to explore new horizons. Sometimes I will seek something adventurous, such as skydiving, and at other times I will seek something simple, such as planting a tree.

4. I will begin to view failure as part of success. If I fail in some way, I will pause and consciously take time to identify what I have learned from the experience. In this way I will learn to see even my defeats as part of the process, as progress.

5. I will examine myself each morning and each evening in the same way that the great spiritual leaders of every tradition have been doing for thousands of years. During my morning assessment, I will ask: *What area do I need to focus on today? What specific action will I take to achieve progress in this area today? How will I measure my progress in this area? What can I do to make a difference in the lives of others today?* Pausing in the evening, I will consciously focus to ask myself: *Am I better today than I was yesterday? What did I do today that brought me happiness? What did I do today that made me restless or unhappy? Why did I choose these things? In what ways can I improve tomorrow? What did I do today to bring happiness to others? Did I harm anyone today physically, emotionally, intellectually, or spiritually? What good things do I feel inspired to do tomorrow?*

Two

_____

Perfectly Imperfect

S ooner or later most of us arrive at a time in our lives where we
say to ourselves, *Something is wrong.* It happens to some people when they are very young and to others when they are much
older. Different circumstances awaken this sense in different people, but it usually is not about the circumstances. The circumstances simply shine a light on it, but they themselves are just
symptoms. The circumstances are external, but the disease is
within.

What we are really saying is, *This is not who I am* or *This is not
who I want to be* or *This is not who I was born to become* or *I don't
feel like myself* or *I don't feel comfortable with myself* or *Who am I,
and what am I here for?* or *I don't like who I've become* or *What is
life really all about—because if this is all there is . . .*

These are all good and valid thoughts and questions.

Sometimes when you get the feeling that something is wrong,
you are mistaken. Something is actually right. Very right. Normal
and healthy. This moment of realizing that something is wrong is

part of the process of maturing into a healthy adult human being. These questions are great questions. Something would be wrong if you never had the courage to ask questions like these.

At these moments of enormous doubt and perplexity, you are waking up. Don't go back to sleep. Don't let someone tell you to just go back to sleep. Embrace this moment. It is the beginning of wonderful new things for you.

Once we arrive at this moment when we sense that something is wrong, a few things could happen. A friend says, "You think too much. You just need to have more of a good time" and proceeds to take you out and get you really drunk. It's just a distraction, but you want to be normal and accepted, so you believe him or her even though there is little if any trace of enduring happiness in his or her own life. The problem with this solution is that it is no solution at all. The next morning, you wake up still feeling that something is wrong, and on top of that, you have a hangover.

We all seem to have moments in which we are especially vulnerable to this phenomenon. A big birthday can send anyone into a tailspin. You tell yourself that your dissatisfaction is due to the fact that you haven't achieved or experienced all you wanted to by this time in your life. So you throw yourself into your work, or a new relationship, with reckless abandon. It's a distraction. You are just avoiding the real issue. You may even be aware of that, but for some reason you can't bring yourself to face it.

I have known people who arrive at this moment of realization who are so seized by a sense of guilt and inadequacy that they immerse themselves in volunteer work or lose themselves in the needs of a child or a spouse. Others put their lives on hold to join the Peace Corps for a year or two to give something back to humankind. These are all good actions in and of themselves, as long as they are being done for the right reason. But in this case,

they are just being used as distractions. And when these people return to their own lives after one, two, or five years, the real questions will still be lingering.

The truth is that when you get the sense that something is
wrong, it may be better to stay exactly where you are and try to
work through whatever it is you are feeling or discovering. What
you don't know is that you are on the brink of a great discovery
about who you are and what you are here for. You are about to discover why you don't like who you have become and what life is really all about. You feel like you are teetering on the edge of a great
abyss, but in fact if you have the courage to jump by standing still,
you will enter deeply into yourself.

At this moment, all you need to do is to stand still and the
whole world will come to you.

But instead of standing still, we prefer a change in job, a new
house, a different lover, an extended vacation, a new car, or any
other change we can think of. We want to delay the real work, distract ourselves from the real questions. If we keep running long
enough, it could take months, years, even decades for these questions to catch up to us again.

Have courage. Be still. Quiet yourself inside and out. Keep
doing what you are doing. Stay where you are. Create some time
for silence and solitude. Don't lie to yourself. Something wonderful is about to happen.

What?

The self-discovery that so many people go off to other places
in search of is right inside us. This discovery of our very *self* leads
us to realize that our imperfections are actually part of our perfection. We are perfectly imperfect. Now this shouldn't become a
blanket excuse for complacency, and so our dilemma lies in working out which aspects of our imperfection are part of who we

really are and which aspects are the result of laziness, self-deception, procrastination, misplaced expectations, conditioning, and past experiences.

All of this leaves us searching for who we really are in ways that are both real and imaginary.

We all have imperfections. Some people have crooked noses, but their crooked noses are part of their perfection. Some people are not well suited for learning foreign languages, but they are perfect without this talent. On the other hand, some people are rude and impatient. This is a defect in character, an imperfection that should be addressed.

The key is to be humble and honest enough to acknowledge which of those imperfections are part of who we are and which are obstacles that stand in the way of being perfectly ourselves. It is a difficult balance, and the self-knowledge required for discerning the difference is acquired little by little along the way. The secret is to apply these truths to our lives as we acquire them. That way the truth will keep coming. Truth lived becomes wisdom, and living in the things we know to be good and true begets further wisdom.

Our perfection is strangely intertwined with our imperfection. It is a mystery that I suspect we will never fully understand, but as we grapple with this mystery, let us celebrate the idea behind the words of the poet Rumi: "Take sips of this pure wine being poured. Don't mind that you've been given a dirty cup."

IT BEGINS WITH A LIE

I don't know if you have noticed, but most of our dilemmas begin with some type of ignorance or deception. Have you ever been told that if you set your mind to it you could achieve anything? That's a lie. For a long time, I believed it. This is the lie that creates the great psychological fault line in the development of young men and women in our society. And once the fault line is there, it's only a matter of time before the earthquake.

Looking back on my childhood, I have identified one consistent and repetitive untruth that I was told. My brothers were misled in the same way, as were my friends. The people who told us this lie thought they were helping us. They wanted only to encourage us. On the surface, it seemed like the good and noble thing to do, but the damage that was being done was below the surface.

The lie has several versions: "You can do anything you set your mind to" and "You can be whatever you want to be as long as you work harder than anyone else" and "You can have anything if you want it bad enough."

At first I was young, and young people tend to believe people who are older and have some kind of authority over them—parents, teachers, coaches, older brothers and sisters, even babysitters. So at first I believed the lie. I set my mind to things and failed. I wanted things badly and failed. And with these failures came feelings of inadequacy and self-loathing, feelings that as a young man I was too proud to talk to anyone about, so I could only bounce them around inside myself without any hope of figuring them out.

In the years since, I have seen this same phenomenon in my brothers and friends, and now I see it in the young people I work with in high schools and colleges.

They apply themselves with all the strength of their will and the focus of desire, and they come up short. Self-doubt begins to plague them. They review the steps they took. They seem sure that they "set their mind to it" as they had been encouraged to do. They did the best they could, but still they failed. They followed those golden maxims set out for them by their teachers, parents, coaches, mentors, professors, and employers . . . and still they fell short.

Sometimes we fail at things because we are simply not well suited to them. But we are seldom told such things when we are young, and our minds are like sponges. People keep telling us that we can do anything if we set our minds to it. These maxims are so absolute and so often reinforced that when we follow them and fail, we are left with only one conclusion: There must be something wrong with me.

Here begins the great wrestle with self-doubt, insecurity, inadequacy, and self-loathing. Many of us struggle with these feelings our whole lives, consciously or subconsciously. Most of us struggle with them semiconsciously. We know that they are there, that they are affecting us, but we don't know what to do with them or about them. These feelings affect our relationships, the way we progress professionally, the way we manage our time, the way we plan for the future, and the way we dream or don't dream.

If the lie is that you can do anything you set your mind to, then what is the truth? Some would say cynically, "You *can't* do anything you set your mind to." But they too would be wrong. The truth is this: We are capable of extraordinary things, but each of us is different. Our unique abilities make us better suited for some things than for others.

What does that mean to you? It means that you can't do anything you set your mind to and that that doesn't make you bad or deficient—just human. It is finding the things that you are better suited for that is one of the great adventures of this life and the source of a great deal of happiness.

You *cannot* do anything you set your mind to. If you are four feet tall, you are not well suited to become the next legendary basketball player. But you are still perfectly suited to be yourself. The real question is this: What are you well suited to achieve and become?

ONLY ONE THING IS ASKED OF YOU

In high school, one of the areas in which I was really able to enjoy myself was art. I loved painting and ceramics, and I loved the stories of the artists that filled the enormous volume of art history that was assigned reading. We didn't read it or study it from cover to cover. We just jumped around, and I loved the liberation from structure that came with that.

I remember feeling uncomfortable jumping around at first. The other teachers had conditioned me. Jumping around didn't seem right. Another piece of bad advice came to mind: "Always finish what you start." And so, I felt a strange guilt for jumping around in this art history text, but it also felt wonderful. The prints intrigued me and led me to wonder about the life and times of the artists behind the art, and so began my fascination with art and the extraordinary personalities that create it.

As I have traveled the world over the years, I have visited art galleries, large and small, in more countries than I can remember. There are, of course, the obvious works to be seen. Several times I have gazed at da Vinci's *Mona Lisa* and stood beneath Michelangelo's *Last Judgment* in the Sistine Chapel with wonder and awe. Every time I go back, I tell myself that this will be the last time—I won't battle with the tourists anymore—but each time, something brings me back. Each time, there is something new and fresh about the experience. I am inspired again and again, and sources of inspiration are irresistible and impossible to ignore.

Matisse, Warhol, Chagall, Monet, van Gogh, Pollock—it's amazing in what cities you find their works around the world. But my favorite artist is Picasso. I'm not entirely certain why, but there is something about his art and about who he was as a person that intrigues me. There are certainly things about the way he lived that are tragic or that I disagree with, but his raw humanity has always fascinated me.

Toward the end of his life, he used to recall in interviews: "When I was a child, my mother used to say to me over and over again, 'Pablo, if you become a soldier you will be a general and if you become a priest you will be Pope.' But I became an artist, and so, I became *Picasso*."

Each and every one of us must make this same journey from the expectations of others to the celebration of self. There is nothing wrong with being a soldier or a priest. But if you were born to become an artist and instead you became a soldier, that would be a tragedy. To become who you were created to be is the only thing that matters and is the only true and lasting success. A woman could become the greatest president her nation has ever seen, but if she were more suited to be a high school teacher, she would feel an inner discomfort her whole life.

It is this inner discomfort that we must identify and root out.

The great challenge is not to succeed but rather to discover what your unique abilities are and offer them to the world in the best way you can. To feel at home with who you are and where you are and what you are doing is worth more than all the treasures and pleasures money can buy. Worldly success and material gain are easy by comparison. The real challenge is not the quest for success but the quest to create inner comfort by being faithful to who we truly are.

In my studies of Judaism, the teachings and stories of Rabbi Zusya have always fascinated me. Wisdom is delivered to all people of all ages by great characters and he was one of them. On one occasion he said, "In the coming world, they will not ask me: 'Why were you not Moses?' They will ask me: 'Why were you not Zusya?' "

"Just be yourself!" How often do we hear this phrase? I love the end of the song "Englishman in New York," when Sting repeats over and over, "Be yourself no matter what they say." We throw the idea around but give little thought as to how very difficult it is to peel back the residue of other people's expectations, past experiences, and the false expectations we have of ourselves.

Only one thing can be reasonably asked of you: that you be yourself. Many people use this as an excuse to indulge in self-destructive behavior or to justify their weaknesses. They proclaim loudly, "This is just who I am!" This is an immaturity that we must all make our way through at some point in our journey. But it is a place to pass through, not a destination from which to live our lives.

Remember this at all times: Being yourself will never lead to your own self-destruction in any manner or degree. Being yourself will never cause you to become a lesser version of yourself. And being yourself means that everything you do and say will help others to become better-versions-of-themselves.

Our Desire to Please

From the moment we are born, we are all searching to understand who we are. The stages of development suggest that at first we take our identity from the people and places that surround us. But as time passes, our own independent identity begins to emerge from within.

We hear stories of "the terrible twos," when children first learn to say no. At first children are simply testing boundaries in order to learn where they are, but even at that very young age, they become quickly aware of their power to manipulate people and situations. The lust for control is born very early. The other period in which we struggle mightily with identity is adolescence, when we begin to dabble with adult choices and assert our independence.

Running parallel to our desire for independence throughout

all stages of development is our desire to please those around us. This desire is born from our need for affirmation, encouragement, and acceptance and the need to belong. We want to be independent, but we also want to be liked and loved. This is natural, but depending on whom we are trying to please and how we are trying to please them, this leaves us wide open to all kinds of psychological distortions. And yet, most of us grow through these periods relatively unscathed, considering the enormity of the risk. But we can be scarred by certain experiences, and we carry the desire to please with us in both healthy and unhealthy ways.

Serving the needs of others is certainly one way to find ourselves, but it can also be a way to lose ourselves. This desire to please one another is part of the indescribable bond among all of the very different members of the human family. But our desire to please and serve should be driven by the needs of others, not by selfish ulterior motives. We should serve others for the sake of service rather than for personal gain.

There are some people we never stop trying to please, for all sorts of healthy and unhealthy reasons, reasons that seem so interwoven with who we are that a whole team of psychologists would struggle to make sense of them. Who is it that we never stop trying to please? For most people, it is their parents or a parent. For others, it can be an early mentor, professional or personal. And for still others, this can include an early lover or a first love.

In my case, it is my parents. As I look back, I see that I have always wanted to please my mother and father, and more than that, I have wanted to impress them. Most of all, I have wanted them to be proud of me. Fortunately, they never placed any pressure or expectations on me in the area of professional or vocational path. When I began speaking and writing, they were not all that supportive at first. I could see that they questioned my decision, thought I was making a mistake, and were worried about me. All of that caused me a great deal of heartache. But again, I was fortunate that the call within was so strong and that by then I had well and truly developed the daily habit of spending time in the classroom of silence to listen to my inner voice.

And yet, there are still days when I am filled with a desire to please my parents. I know that they love me deeply, but I want them to be proud of me in a way that parents have never been proud of a son. Even now, I still want to please my dead father, want him to be proud of me. There are moments that I have to stop myself and remind myself how much he loved me and how pleased he was toward the end of his life with how I have chosen to spend mine. And still I yearn for an ounce more certainty.

Experience has taught me that I am not alone in all of this. One of my passions is for movies. I don't care much for television, but I love good movies that draw me out of my own little world, expanding my vision of myself and my vision of the world. One of my all-time favorite lines is from the Robert Redford movie *The Natural.* Redford plays a forty-year-old rookie, Roy Hobbs, who helps a flailing New York team win the pennant.

Toward the end of the movie, the coach is talking to one of the assistant coaches about how his mother always told him he should be a farmer. The coach must have been in his late sixties or early seventies, and still he was thinking about what his mother thought he should do with his life. The coach then goes on to say that if they had won the pennant he would have walked away from the game and bought a farm.

Hobbs is standing behind the coaches, watching them shave and listening to this conversation. "There's nothing like a farm," he says with a smile to make them aware of his presence. Coach looks up at him in the mirror without turning around and says, "My mother always said I should be a farmer."

Hobbs's smile fades and he casts his eyes down for a moment

as if remembering something from long ago, then looking up with all the conviction of destiny, he says, "My dad wanted me to be a baseball player."

It's amazing how much sway our mother wanting us to be a lawyer or a doctor or our father wanting us to be a teacher or a baseball player can have over the rest of our lives. I tell you all this to illustrate the strong emotional ties we carry with us throughout our lives and the enormous burden other people's expectations can be.

Part of the process of self-discovery is developing a desire to please and serve other people in healthy ways. I know parents who still clean, shop, wash, and in some cases, make beds for their grown children. It's unhealthy for the children and the parents. It creates a situation of control and codependency that ultimately negatively impacts their relationship with one another and their ability to be authentically themselves. On the other hand, I know parents who have flown across the country in emergency situations to take care of an adult child who was ill, and this became the birth of a new and deeper relationship between parent and child.

It is also important to remember that what is healthy for you might be unhealthy for someone else. Volunteering to organize an auction at your child's school or to help with child care at your church may be very healthy for you, but on top of everything else that someone else has on her plate, it might be unhealthy for her. Some things are unhealthy by their very nature; other things are unhealthy when they are added to everything else we have going on. Sometimes good things are bad for *you*.

There are several litmus tests that help us determine whether our desire to serve is healthy. We can begin by examining our motives. Why are we thinking of doing it? Is it out of a sense of obligation or guilt, or do we genuinely feel called to help in this way?

Is it going to help the other person become the best-version-of-themselves? Is it going to help you become the-best-version-of-yourself? If we have been asked to do something, who asked us, and what were their motives for asking? Another powerful method of discernment is to listen to your body. When you think about what is before you, do you get a lighthearted feeling or a heavy, oppressive feeling? Finally, ask yourself, how will you feel when you are finished doing whatever it is you are considering?

We can go too far in either direction, and as with most things, the answer lies somewhere in the middle. Some people refuse to serve others at all and get completely absorbed in a world of self. Others get so caught up in serving that they lose sight of who they are. We all have a great need to serve, to make a contribution. In my own quest for happiness, I like to remind myself that I know a lot of very selfish people, but I don't know any selfish people who are happy. Learning to serve others in healthy ways is part of maturing as a human being. We simply need to find a healthy balance.

Our desire to please is innate. Ultimately we must decide who our audience is going to be—our parents, children, friends, colleagues, boss, critics, spouse, self, God. We have all known people who try to please everyone and end up completely miserable themselves. Who is your audience?

ARE YOU HAPPY?

Really. Think about it for a moment. Don't just float over the question like any other words on a page. Are you happy?

Since I have started asking the question in my seminars, people have started asking me the question. At first I would always say yes, either because that was what they wanted to hear or because I felt I had to be. But I noticed that sometimes it felt inauthentic. Sometimes I wasn't happy. So I started to pause when people asked me and really take my temperature, so to speak, and answer meaningfully.

For most people the answer is "Yes and no" or "Yes, but I could be happier." There are very few people, perhaps none, who have no happiness in their lives. But there are also very few people, perhaps none, who have no unhappiness in their lives.

Some people are unhappy because they don't like their job or their spouse. Others are unhappy because they don't know how to relax or appreciate who they are and all they have. Some people are desperately unhappy because of a chemical imbalance in their brains. I have seen it. It is real and tragic. But most of us experience unhappiness when we wander away from ourselves.

Unhappiness is the fruit of doing and saying things that contradict who we are and what we are here for. Unhappiness is not something that happens to us as if we are poor little victims. Unhappiness is something we do to ourselves. You can choose to be happy.

People have chosen to be happy in worse circumstances than you or I will ever likely find ourselves in. No one has demonstrated that more than Viktor Frankl did in *Man's Search for Meaning* as he recalled his experiences in Nazi concentration camps during World War II. Over and over, he encountered people who even though they were starving would share their inadequate rations with others. Frankl explains that while some were killing themselves or wallowing in self-pity, others were filled with an inexplicable happiness, a real joy that was independent of substance or circumstances. Their happiness did not depend on favorable external circumstances but had its source within.

What causes your unhappiness?

Are you burdened by expectations that you have placed on yourself? Are these expectations healthy and real, or are they unhealthy illusions? Do you tell yourself that other people have placed these expectations on you? Do you tell yourself that other people cause your unhappiness? That if they would only do what they are supposed to do, then you would be happy? Is the whole world out of place, or are you out of place? Perhaps it's simpler for you than that. Maybe it's your job, your spouse, your boss, or your children.

There are an unlimited number of ways and reasons to be unhappy at this very moment. Unhappiness is always an option, but so is happiness.

But what is happiness? It is not easily defined, but we all know it when we experience it. I have often wondered what Thomas Jefferson thought happiness was when he wrote, in the Declaration of Independence, "We hold these truths to be self-evident, that all men are created equal, that they are endowed by their Creator with certain inalienable Rights, that among these are Life, Liberty and the pursuit of Happiness."

Let me tell you about my experiences with happiness and her ugly twin sister unhappiness.

The first thing I learned is that you will never be happy pretending to be someone other than yourself. On too many occasions to count, and in ways too embarrassing to recall, I have tried to impress people by pretending to be someone other than who I really am. The gentle voice within cried out to advise me that I was betraying myself, but I ignored it. The result was that I felt very uncomfortable in my own skin, and the outcome was never what I had foolishly convinced myself that it would be.

Most people can spot someone pretending to be other than who they really are as easily as they can spot a teenager looking to be the center of attention or a man wearing shoes that are four sizes too big. If we are to be happy, it will be as ourselves.

The second thing that I learned is that pleasure and happiness are not synonymous. The difference and distinction between the two is subtle but real.

Pleasure cannot be sustained beyond the experience producing it. You eat, and you experience pleasure. You stop eating, and the pleasure stops. That's why we don't stop eating. We're not hungry; we enjoy the pleasure that comes from eating. We have disconnected eating from the function that allows us to fuel our incredible bodies and have turned eating into a pastime. The same is true for so many of the pleasures of this world.

Happiness is different. Happiness can be sustained beyond the experience producing it. Take, for example, exercising or working out. You come home from work, and it is your day to work out. Now, you don't really feel like working out, so you have to make a choice. Are you going to plant yourself in your recliner chair in front of your 127-inch idiot box with a 300-ounce bag of potato chips, or are you going to work out? The choice is yours. The question is: Which will bring you happiness? Some would say watching television and eating potato chips, but they would be confusing pleasure for real and lasting happiness.

Think back to other times when you have not felt like working out. Some of those times, you probably chose the recliner chair, potato chips, and television. Did it make you happy? How did you feel three or four hours later? Refreshed and rejuvenated? I think not. How did you feel about yourself?

On the other hand, think about the times when you don't feel like working out, but you do it anyway. Once you get done working out, you're always glad you did, aren't you? And the sense of satisfaction and well-being lasts for hours after you are finished working out. That's happiness. Happiness can be sustained beyond the activity producing the happiness.

Too often we judge an activity by how we feel about it beforehand. This is a failed notion. We should not judge activities by how we feel about them beforehand; we should judge them by how we feel in retrospect.

In every moment of our lives, we choose between happiness and misery. And sometimes long-term misery comes disguised as short-term pleasure. Sooner or later, most of us realize that our desire for happiness is much more than a desire for pleasure, and that pleasure will not quench our desire for happiness. Some of us are slower learners than others, but in time most people come to the discovery that their yearning is for lasting happiness in a changing world. Sadly, many form serious and lifelong addictions before they come to these realizations and spend the rest of their lives as slaves to pleasure.

We yearn for a happiness that can be sustained independently of substances—food, drink, drugs—and a happiness that can be sustained independently of circumstances—success, money, possessions, opportunities, weather, and so on.

Happiness is an inside job and has very little to do with substances, money, possessions, pleasure, or circumstances.

The third realization that I have come to in my own pursuit of happiness is that the philosophy of popular culture is deeply flawed. Our culture propagates the idea that if you go out and get what you want, then you will be happy. For fifty years, this has been the dominant philosophy, and people have been going out and getting what they want on an ever-increasing basis. But look around. There is no evidence in our society to suggest that people are happier today than they were fifty years ago. In fact, the exact opposite is in evidence. People seem more irritable, restless, and discontented than ever before. Suicide rates and incidence of depression are reaching epidemic levels, and yet we continue to chant this philosophy as the great cure-all of our age.

The philosophy of "go out and get what you want" is a failed experiment, but we keep telling ourselves that when we get what we want, and enough of what we want, then we will be happy. The reason it doesn't work is because you simply never can get enough of what you don't really need. Getting what you want won't necessarily make you happy. You have to want the right things. Happiness is born when we begin to want and seek what we truly need.

My fourth and final realization has been this: Happiness cannot be found by pursuing happiness. That's a staggering idea. It is an idea that most of us either refuse to ponder or refuse to believe. But it is one of the great truths in our quest for enduring happiness. If you set out to find and have happiness, it will elude you at every turn. If you turn happiness into an end in and of itself, you will never have it. Happiness is not an end or even an experience. Happiness is a by-product.

Happiness is not achieved by the pursuit of happiness but rather by right living. My friend Tony says to me over and over again, "Just do the next right thing!" In every situation, at every juncture, at all crossroads, simply do the next right thing.

If the choice at this moment is between exercising or vegetating in front of the television, just do the next right thing. If the choice is between cheating on your wife or being faithful to her, just do the next right thing. If the choice is between working well and working hard or being lazy and procrastinating, just do the next right thing.

Some may argue that these examples are very simple and ask, "What about when I have to choose between helping my child with his homework or helping my spouse with the dishes?" or "How do I decide between going after a promotion that will give me enough money to send my kids to college or taking a job that I love but will limit their choices when it comes to colleges?" The questions life throws at us can sometimes involve many shades of gray. The thing we have to remember is that we have to make only one decision at a time. The best way to prepare for the future is to make the right decision now. Will you make the wrong choice sometimes? Sure. We all do. But most of the time, if we take a gut check—pause to listen to the quiet voice within us—we are going to get it right.

By doing the next right thing, we live on into the answers to the questions that we could not answer before, because it was not time to answer them. Who is to know what you are to do a month from now, or a year from now, or ten years from now? But if at every moment you occupy yourself with doing the next right thing—the thing that will help you become a-better-version-of-yourself right now—then when the time comes, you will find yourself dealing with the decisions that perplex you today in the same calm and knowing way. Don't make decisions today that are not called for until next week, next month, or next year. Make good decisions today in the matters you have to decide today.

Nothing brings happiness like right living. Think of that gentle voice within you. We all have one. Some call it conscience. Call it whatever you want to, but we all have it. I like to think of it as the-best-version-of-myself talking to me, pleading with me to let him come to life. This voice within us wants desperately to lead us to happiness, but too often we ignore it or turn our back on the path it suggests. Let me ask you a question. When was the last time you lived by what that gentle voice within you suggested and the outcome was unhappiness? When did that voice ever lead you to betray yourself?

The pursuit of happiness means different things to different people. It means different things to you and me at different stages in our journey. Some people seem more naturally disposed to happiness. They tend toward gratitude. Others seem more disposed to being irritable, restless, and discontented.

I must confess I consider myself among the latter. I have to work hard each day to create a disposition of gratitude. I often tend toward the cynical and pessimistic. With no effort or conscious thought, I can be irritable, restless, and discontented. I was probably not always like this, and no doubt, I have done something to form these tendencies. I probably wasn't born with them, but I live with them every day. Perhaps in this I am just harsh on myself, as I am in so many other things.

Some people just seem happy on the outside but are desperately sad within. I dated a woman like that once. She was spectacularly beautiful, confident, intelligent, and funny—perfect in so many ways. She was always smiling and laughing and making other people laugh and smile. But as I got to know her, I came to learn that it was all just a façade. Deep inside she harbored a whole world of fear and hurt.

Happiness is a lot like wealth and wisdom: Those who have it generally don't need to talk about it, and those who are constantly talking about it usually don't have it. You know when you've got it and you know when you don't, but do you know what creates it? The nine lessons for enduring happiness provide practical and powerful insights about how we can create lasting happiness in this changing world. They do not form an oppressive program of "do this and do that" but rather offer suggestions about how to approach life one day at a time.

A CHANCE TO TURN IT ALL AROUND

I often end my e-mails with the last words from one of my earlier works: "Something wonderful is about to happen!"

People often ask me how I can be filled with such great hope, knowing the challenges that face humanity and having seen and experienced so much of the world. My reasons for hope are very simple. In the first place, I believe that people are innately good. For the most part, it has been my experience that people will good for other people; they want good things to happen to you and me. The second reason is because I believe in our capacity for change and growth. Many people don't believe that people can change, but I have seen men and woman emerge from patterns of failure and addictive behaviors that seemed beyond hope; and in these men and woman I have witnessed the miracle of human transformation. My third reason for hope is because I know that every moment is another chance to turn it all around.

A couple of weeks ago I received a letter from a woman who had been reading my books and had come across the line "Something wonderful is about to happen!" Of the thousands of pieces of correspondence I receive, from time to time a note, a letter, or an e-mail will provide an extension that is exhilarating. In her letter, she simply wanted to observe that while it was good and healthy to have hope for the future, we shouldn't overlook the fact that something wonderful *is* happening.

The something wonderful that is happening is this very moment. There is no opportunity or teacher like the moment we are in right now. Brimming with possibilities, the present moment wants to be seized, enjoyed, exercised, and squeezed for every last drop it has to offer.

The thing about moments is that they don't always come at a convenient time. Moments arrive unannounced. Important moments are particularly difficult to predict. The only real way to be prepared for both the great and difficult moments of life is to be constantly practicing present-moment awareness.

Present-moment awareness can be achieved in any number of simple ways. You may decide that you are simply going to ask yourself over and over again, *What can I do right now that will help me to become more perfectly myself?* If that were the mantra of your inner dialogue, over time you would become a master of present-moment awareness and participation.

Too often we spend our days and weeks wishing our lives away, waiting for some future experience that we have fantasized will erase all of our problems and make us happy. In the meantime we are missing out on life, moment by moment.

The thing I love most about moments is that moments are manageable. I can manage a moment. Days, weeks, months, and years seem like eternities sometimes. If I tell myself I'm not going to eat any chocolate for a month, I begin to obsess over it. But if, when the cravings for chocolate begin to speak to me, I tell myself, *Not right now*, I can handle that. In this way moments play a powerful role in teaching us how to make and celebrate progress.

The other wonderful thing about moments is that they provide glimpses of the-best-version-of-ourselves. There are moments in each day that I can look back on and honestly say, "For that moment I was perfectly myself." Not many, but some. In those moments I know I could not have handled myself any better. The more I acknowledge and celebrate those moments, and the more I seek to understand what allowed me to thrive in those moments, the more I find myself repeating them.

Think about it. In what moments over the past week or two were you at your very best? What were the contributing factors? How can you increase the number of those moments?

These moments provide the clues that tell us which path leads to the place where we are at peace with who we are, where we are, and what we are doing. Once we are at peace with ourselves in this way, it is amazing how much easier it is to see the good in everyone and everything. It is then that we are flooded with a simple gratitude for life that allows our spirits to soar.

I would be remiss also if I did not acknowledge the role that the moment plays in our success in any field. All success has its root in being able to capitalize on the moment, endure the moment, and draw from the moment what is to be learned, gained, or achieved.

Here on my desk in my study where I write, I have an hour-glass. I turn it on its head, and it empties the sand out in a perfect hour. Several years ago, I was walking through the streets of Rome with my friend Gaia when I saw it in the window of a famous toy store just off the edge of Piazza Navona. As soon as I saw it, I knew exactly what I wanted it for and where I wanted to place it.

You may wonder why it is such a powerful tool for me. The reason is that in a sense, time is always being lost. You never find time. Time is either used wisely or wasted foolishly. We wear watches and look at clocks. Their hands go around and around or they have digital numbers that renew themselves with the same frequency. All of this creates the illusion that time is constantly there. It gives the impression that time is circular. It is not. Time is linear. Once it has passed, it has passed.

It seems that someone is always making a new movie version of H. G. Wells's novel *The Time Machine*. In more recent versions the emphasis seems to be placed on this message: You cannot change one moment of the past, so grasp the present moment and change the future. There is power in this moment. Use it, direct it, harness it. Moments are like the petals of a rose; they fall to the ground if there is no life in them.

FROM CONFUSION TO CLARITY

We seem to spend endless hours planning and worrying about some distant future that is promised to none of us, and yet effort-lessly overlook the fact that how we deal with the here and now will determine what the future looks like. In financial language, the lesson is: Take care of the pennies, and the dollars will take care of themselves. In the language of life and time, the lesson is much the same.

When I am frustrated, angry, confused, or distracted, I often call my good friend Tony. He always asks me the same question: "So what's going on?" Then he gives me the chance to vent a little. I think he has long sensed that I need people in my life who allow me to vent and has heroically offered himself to me in this way. Once I am done ranting about whatever is getting me down, he usually offers the very same simple piece of advice: Just do the next right thing.

He says it to me over and over again. I say it to myself over and over again. And still I need to hear it over and over again. It's amazing how quickly things can be turned around for the better if we just focus on doing the next right thing. Maybe that means exercising, or maybe it means apologizing. It might mean stepping beyond the excuses and procrastination and throwing ourselves into our work or a project. It may just mean eating a good, healthy meal or calling your mother.

One reason doing the next right thing can change things so quickly is because very often, whatever we think the problem is or whatever is getting us down is imagined. It's different in our minds than it is in reality, because we have a tendency to distort and exaggerate. Another reason doing the next right thing can change our state so quickly is because it immediately gets us moving in the direction of progress. And when we are making progress, we feel better about ourselves and better about life.

Sometimes people will say to me, "But what if you don't know what the next right thing is?" The truth is that we almost always do. More than ninety-nine percent of the time, you will know what the next right thing for you to do is if you quiet yourself for a moment and go to that place deep within you. You will know what you can and should do right now to become a-better-version-of-yourself. The other one percent of the time, you may have to turn to a trusted friend to help you figure out the right thing, but if you are committed to doing the next right thing, you will find it.

The real beauty of focusing on immediate actions is that it lifts the clouds of confusion. We all feel confused at times, but we are rarely confused about what we should be doing right now. Just do the next right thing, and you'll see how uncannily clear the next step will become. Clarity is delivered moment by moment.

Just do the next right thing! This is the message that our inner self wants to cry out to us over and over throughout our lives. One step leads to another. Interim steps cannot be skipped. Embrace the now, and the future will be richer and more abundant because you had the wisdom, courage, and discipline to embrace this moment.

The second lesson for enduring happiness is this:

JUST DO THE NEXT RIGHT THING.

Whether you are struggling to overcome a pattern of defeat, yearning for inner peace, trying to create lasting happiness, wishing to succeed in your career, desperately trying to overcome procrastination, or are battling with an addiction, this lesson holds the key for you. Just do the next right thing. In each moment, just keep doing the next right thing.

You cannot think your way out or talk your way out of these problems. You acted your way into them, and you must act your way out of them. You must act in the sense of action, not in the sense of pretense. It is purposeful action that will lead you to become a-better-version-of-yourself, and action is the key to progress.

Whenever you get into a funk, just do the next right thing. And keep doing the next right thing. You will be amazed at how quickly you work yourself out of the funk if you approach it in this way. Don't worry about next week or next month or next year. Just do the next right thing and keep doing the next right thing, and gradually you will act your way out of destructive patterns. You cannot think or pray or wish or hope yourself out of the pattern that is holding you back. You must act your way out of it, one moment at a time.

One moment at a time, by simply doing the next right thing, you will move from confusion to clarity, from misunderstanding to insight, from despair to hope, from darkness to light, and discover your truest self.

Applying the Second Lesson for
Enduring Happiness:

JUST DO THE NEXT RIGHT THING

I will apply the second lesson of enduring happiness
to my life by taking the following steps:

1. In every moment and in every circumstance, I will do whatever I honestly believe to be the next right thing. I will ask myself throughout the day, especially when I find myself distracted, unfocused, or idle, *What can I do right now that will help me to become more perfectly myself?* Once I have determined what the next right thing is, I will act without hesitation.

2. I will consult with my inner self in all decisions, pausing when necessary to reflect on what the best course of action is for the situation at hand. I will learn to take note when I am experiencing inner comfort or discomfort. I will remind myself that the best decisions we make, and the only ones we never regret, are made from a place deep within ourselves.

3. I will participate more fully in each moment by practicing present-moment awareness. I will actively seek the lessons and opportunities that each moment wants to bestow on me. In each moment I will make myself present and available to the people, places, and activities at hand.

4. I will choose happiness as my emotional default position. When I choose unhappiness, I will do so to heal myself of any hurt that I have experienced. In these moments I will not resist unhappiness but rather will surrender to it, immersing myself in it as a path to healing. I will become consciously aware of the people, actions, thoughts, places, and things that contribute to my happiness or unhappiness. Over time I will begin to take note of who and what consistently make me happy.

5. I will abandon the ideal of perfection that focuses on external appearances in favor of the perfection that is concerned with character, integrity, and the inner reality. I will remain mindful of the fact that being perfectly myself always leads me along the path toward the-best-version-of-myself. I will seek honestly to determine which aspects of my imperfection are part of who I am and which aspects stem from a defect in my character. At every crossroad, I will remind myself that my only obligation is to be myself.

Three

Looking Into the Future

If we are sincere about wanting to improve ourselves and the world we live in, do we know what will bring about this progress? Do we really believe that money and an ever-increasing economic standard of living will solve our problems or bring us happiness? Can politics negotiate the change we so desire for our lives and our world?

There are probably many things that can bring about the progress we desire, but the approach I find most compelling is the one suggested by Occam's razor: that we allow the simplest answer to guide us. What is the simplest solution to the problems we face? What factor will most affect the change we desire? What is the one thing that can most bring about genuine progress in our lives and in society at large?

The answer is character. Character will affect your future more than any other single ingredient. Character is the best preparation for every scenario. Character is the best investment you can make in your future and the future of humanity. Character is the simple answer, but it would be a mistake to confuse *simple* with *easy*.

CAN YOU SEE INTO THE FUTURE?

"Let's talk about your future." Did your parents or teachers ever say this to you? People very often become obsessed with making the unknown future known but usually overlook the key indicators.

Would you like to be able to see into the future? Some people say they would, and others say they would prefer not to. Different responses are driven by different motives. Some want to see into the future so that if they see something they don't like, they can do something about it. Others don't want to see into the future, because they believe if they saw something they didn't like, they would have no power to change it.

The reality is that to a certain extent, we can see into the future, and we can do something about it if we see something we don't like in our future. Thoughts create actions. Actions create habits. Habits create character. And your character is your destiny—in the workplace and in relationships. In every sphere of life, your character provides significant insight into your future.

At the core of character we find our habits. Character is not what someone says but what he or she actually does. Habits are the building blocks of character. What are your habits? What are the things you do every day, every week, or every month? If you can tell me what your habits are, I can tell you what your future looks like. The future is not something that happens to us. It is an external expression of our internal reality.

We can see into the future. If *your* character is *your* destiny, what does *your* future look like? The danger in answering this question is that we may be tempted to isolate one trait in our character and rush to judgment about our future on the basis of that one detail. Some of us tend to rush toward something negative, and others tend to rush toward something positive. But we are more complicated than that. Some of the habits that make up our character point to happy and prosperous futures; others signify misery somewhere down the road. We need to be honest with ourselves and take both the positive and negative aspects of our characters into account. It is easy to fixate on one or two aspects of our character and ignore the rest. Focusing on such a small part of who we are can really skew what we discover. One way to avoid this pitfall is to ask others what they consider to be the strengths and weaknesses of our character. The people around us often see things that we cannot see ourselves.

The good news is that whatever we discover, we can change our habits and can improve our character. If we don't like what we see when we look into the future through the telescope of character, we can change the future. How? By changing our habits. Our lives change when our habits change. It is true that if you tell me what your habits are today, I can tell you what your future looks like. If you tell me what new habits you are going to put into place this year, I can tell you how your life will be different this year from what it was last year.

If you looked into your future and saw trials and heartache or triumph and glory, how would you prepare for your future? The reality is that you are likely to face all of these things in the future to varying degrees and at moments when you least expect them. The best way to prepare for the unexpected is to start building character.

Character is the best preparation for every situation.

BETTER LIVES, BETTER FUTURES

For thousands of years, people have been asking the same questions. The circumstances and technologies of our lives may have changed, but the essence of the human struggle has not, because our essential purpose is common and unchanging. Each of us is here to become the-best-version-of-ourselves. The particular situations and circumstances we encounter are just opportunities to live out this purpose. The problems we experience are there not so much to be solved as to help you become your best self. The questions our hearts struggle with today are the same questions that people struggled with a thousand years ago. Aristotle and Socrates grappled with the very same concerns that you and I grapple with today.

This is the first of those timeless questions: Is it better to live well or to live for a long time? We may never have articulated this question and taken time to reflect on it, but it is important nonetheless. Most reasonable people would agree that it is better to live well, at least in theory. Faced with death or old age, many may hesitate a little. Of course, we could probably all disagree about what it means to live well, but that is part of what we are driving at here. For some people living well means having money and possessions; for some it means being a contributing member of society; for some it means having opportunities; for some it means abiding by a moral code; for some it simply means having fun or enjoying good health.

What does living well mean for you?

If we wish to improve our lives, we must know first what will produce the improvement we desire. From my own experience, I know that money and opportunities can improve our lives, but only to a very limited extent, one that is often massively overstated.

The quality of our lives is most powerfully changed when we grow in character.

Popular culture seems much more interested in celebrity and talent than it is with character. Role models and heroes are almost exclusively selected on the basis of talent and celebrity status. Whether the celebrity actually possesses any qualities worthy of emulation doesn't appear to be one of the criteria in the selection process. In ways small and large, we become our role models and heroes. We become the people we admire. And if that is true, shouldn't we all be a little concerned about where this trend might be taking us?

We seem more interested in a person's talent than we are with how he handles himself as a person. Have we overlooked the bare truth that talent is something we are born with? Granted, it takes hard work and dedication to bring talent to its full fruition, but most extraordinarily talented people are born with a capacity in a certain area that the rest of us are not born with. They sharpen the knife, but the knife was given to them.

The other great truth here is that talent is limited. Your ability to improve on the talents you have been given is almost limitless, but you cannot increase the *number* or *type* of talents you have. They are generic or God-given. You are born with talents. You either have them or you don't. If you have no talent for singing, you can't sing and you won't develop the talent. You may take lesson after lesson, but you will not be able to sing. If you are a poor singer and take lesson after lesson and become a good singer, that means that the talent was there. It may have been lying below the surface, waiting to be discovered, but it was already there. Trying different activities helps us to discover our talents so that we can nurture them. That's why a well-rounded education includes exposure to many different areas and disciplines.

But while talent is limited, your ability to increase your character is virtually unlimited. So why do we spend so much time focusing on talent and so little time developing character?

If we truly wish to improve our lives and our world, we need to switch the focus from what we have and what we do to who we are and who we are becoming. Our obsession with talent and celebrity, with money and possessions, is distracting us from the real source of fulfillment and satisfaction in this life: character.

Character is a gift that you give to yourself, and it is one of the few things that can never be taken from you.

WHAT DO YOU RESPECT?

I have had an extraordinary life. Sometimes when people ask me about my day or what's been happening in my life lately, I start speaking, and then they get this look of amazement on their face. Then I start listening to myself, and I realize that what is an ordinary day or week for me staggers the imagination of most people. My life is not better or worse than yours, just different. And just as much as some people long for a taste of the extraordinary elements of my life, I can assure you I long for the ordinary elements of their lives in the same way from time to time.

People always ask me what my favorite places are in the more than fifty countries I have traveled to. I have many favorites, but as I reflect on why they are my favorites, I discover that it is the people I know in those places that attracts me to them. When you have traveled as much as I have, you come to realize that it is not where you are but who you are with that matters most.

Over the years I have met literally hundreds of thousands of people, but as I look back on it all, there are certain people whom I remember, others whom I admire, and a handful whom I deeply respect. Some people are memorable because they are so warm and welcoming, and others because they make you laugh until you have cramps in your cheeks. There are people I remember simply because they happened to be there at a moment when something wonderful or tragic took place. Then there are the people I admire.

I admire people for so many different reasons. I admire people who take care of themselves physically, because I know how hard it is to do that. Some people make the excuse that it doesn't come naturally to them. I don't think a finely tuned body comes naturally to anyone. When I watch the Olympics and I see the athletes' extraordinary bodies, I know that they are the result of extraordinary discipline, and I admire that.

I admire great talent. Musicians, artists, writers, actors, athletes, teachers, scientists, and spiritual leaders, all exercising their talents on an extraordinary level, fascinate me, and I admire that.

I admire the building of great businesses and wealth. It is something that has intrigued me from a very young age. Many of my best friends are business leaders and entrepreneurs, and I often marvel at the way their minds work. I also admire people who have worked hard all their lives, saved hard, invested wisely and consistently, and amassed a small fortune. I admire that.

But over the years in my personal reflection, I have constantly asked myself: *What do I respect?* And at a deep level, I think there is only one thing I truly and deeply respect over and over again in time, and that is virtue. I respect virtue. Virtue inspires me. Virtue in other people challenges me. Virtue raises me up. Virtue allows me to catch a glimpse of what is possible. Virtue gives me hope for the future of humanity.

When I see virtue in the life of a man or woman, my first response is to want to spend more time with that person. But I have also noticed that there are times when people of virtue repel me. There are times when I avoid them. On reflection, I realize that it is at these times that I am neglecting the call to progress, have stopped along the way to indulge in some self-destructive behavior or another, and their mere presence challenges me to get back on the path and embrace my authentic self.

The thing that strikes me most about people of virtue, genuine virtue, is that whether I like them or dislike them as individuals, whether I agree with them or disagree with them ideologically, I cannot help but respect them.

Character is built one habit at a time. Good character is built one virtue at a time. Virtue is a good habit, a habit that leads us to become the-best-version-of-ourselves. The cornerstone of character is virtue.

Character is at the very core of our happiness. Patient people are more likely to experience enduring happiness than impatient people. Generous and grateful people are more likely to create sustainable happiness in their lives than those who are ungrateful and greedy. I have never met people with unforgiveness in their heart who were truly and deeply happy. People who can forgive are happier than those who hold grudges and harbor unforgiveness. The gentle seem more likely to experience happiness than the rough and angry. Moderation is a more likely path to enduring happiness than gluttony and lust. Kindness will bring us a happiness that will outshine the pleasure of self-indulgence every time.

Ask yourself these simple questions: Would you rather live next door to a man who is kind and thoughtful or to a man who is mean and self-centered? Would you rather work for a woman who is honest and caring or for a woman who is dishonest, conniving, and uncaring? Would you rather be married to someone who is grateful, patient, and generous or to someone who is ungrateful, impatient, and self-seeking? Would you rather have friends with integrity or friends who cannot be trusted to do as they say they will do?

I would rather be surrounded by virtuous people, because

their joy for life and their virtue are contagious. Their mere presence helps me to become the-best-version-of-myself.

Our culture has reduced all virtue to the universal virtue of niceness, which is no virtue at all. People comment, "Oh, she is such a nice woman" or "He is such a nice man," which in essence very often means that this man or woman never says or does anything to upset the person making the comment, never ruffles any feathers, never challenges anyone to rise to greater virtue. In a way this person is a nonperson who is admired for being so—for not getting in the way. I hope nobody who knows me ever describes me as "nice" in this context. I hope to upset the people around me occasionally, to rattle them from time to time, to challenge them in ways that make them feel uneasy. For if I do not from time to time cross the line of niceness with the people close to me, then I am almost certainly not the son, brother, friend, employer, colleague, citizen, or man that I aspire to be.

Love makes demands upon us. To love someone means that from time to time you will be required by that love to tell someone something that they would rather not hear. Forthrightness is one of the fundamental elements of healthy relationships, and yet most people lack the virtue to challenge the people they claim to love in this way. The most obvious example of this is in modern parenting. Many parents seem more interested in being a friend to their children than in being a parent. Their children don't need another friend; they need their parents. In seeking this acceptance and approval from their children, many parents shrink back from the corrective element of parenting and do not serve as a guide to their children.

I see a similar situation often among high school teachers who shirk the responsibility entrusted to them in the area of discipline, merely to be popular with their students.

We have mistaken niceness for virtue. Niceness is not virtue.

As I travel the world speaking to audiences, I get the growing sense that people feel that something is missing. For a time many of us sensed that something was simply missing in our lives as individuals. But of late, it seems more and more people are awakening to the fact that something is missing in society on a larger scale. Though most are unable to articulate it, more and more people are filled with the sense that we have collectively lost or forgotten something.

They are right. We have lost something. We did leave something behind. In our obsession with change, we overlooked the fundamental truth that progress is change that makes our lives and society better. Our lives genuinely improve in a way that can be sustained only when we grow in virtue. Individual virtues are the bricks that build character, and character is the backbone of all authentic progress for individuals, communities, cultures, and societies.

What do I respect? I respect virtue. What do you respect?

ARE YOU TRUSTWORTHY?

If it is virtue that causes our lives and society to improve, then we must ask the question "What does it mean to be virtuous?" Harry Emerson Fosdick wrote, "No virtue is more universally accepted as a test of good character than trustworthiness." First and foremost, to be a man or woman of virtue is about honesty and truth, honesty with self and others, and an insatiable hunger to know and live truth.

Rigorous honesty and love of truth in turn give birth to integrity. Honesty means that we can be taken at our word and that what we say can be trusted. Integrity means that we can be relied on to do what we say we will do. Together, honesty and integrity make us worthy of trust—trustworthy. As George Washington once said, "I hope I shall always possess firmness and virtue enough to maintain what I consider the most enviable of all titles, the character of the 'Honest Man.' "

But honesty is no easy feat today. It seems that we celebrate an honesty of convenience, in which a certain amount of lying and deception is deemed necessary. We are honest when it doesn't cost us anything, but the moment we are called on to sacrifice something to be honest, we abandon this virtue.

We are taught honesty of convenience in many ways from a very early age. I remember that when I was a child, my older brothers would take us to the movies. Just before we went to buy our tickets, they would tell me how old I was that day. If I was eleven but there was a child's price for children ten and younger, then I automatically became ten. It's a small thing, but it is dishonest, and children learn such lessons very quickly.

Little by little this honesty of convenience has crept into our lives and become an accepted norm in our society. Rigorous honesty is a very hard thing to find.

But if we are being dishonest with others, we are also being dishonest with ourselves. The external reality is an expression of the internal reality: We must lie to ourselves before we lie to anyone else. And that is a betrayal of self.

The first step is to be honest with ourselves, but we willingly and consciously deceive ourselves in so many ways. We tell ourselves that we have to do what we do, that there are no other options. We tell ourselves that we have to live where we live. We tell ourselves that if our spouse wasn't the way he or she is, then we wouldn't be in the place we are emotionally. We tell ourselves that our partner will change. We tell ourselves that we have to feel what we are feeling. If we are victims of anything, we are victims of our own self-deception.

Be honest with yourself. Is that relationship really going anywhere? Why do you spend so much money and save so little? Do you really need to go on another diet or instead learn to enjoy food in moderation? If you could do anything with your life, what would you do? Why would you do that? How often do you really exercise? Do you regularly spend time in the classroom of silence to work out who you are and what you are here for? What are you really good at? What good things do you feel inspired to do? What is one thing that you could do that would dramatically impact your life for the better? Are you earnestly pursuing your dreams?

We tell ourselves lies about ourselves, about our work, our spouses, our children, and any number of other people and situations: "Everything would be great if I lost weight (or quit my job or found the perfect partner)." "He really loves me; he's just afraid to commit." "I just couldn't say no." "I could quit if I really wanted to." "I don't need help." "I'm not lost." "If I had more time, I'd exercise more (or write a book or go back to school or spend more time with my family)." "She cheated on him, but she would never cheat on me."

Why do we lie to ourselves? Perhaps it is because the truth is too much to face or because we lack the courage to act on the truth we know we are avoiding. We tell ourselves lies in a distorted attempt to remain sane, but in fact it is the lies that turn us toward insanity.

Being honest with ourselves is at the very core of integrity. It is the first step. Honesty with self is what makes honesty with others possible. Do you ever sit and listen to someone saying something completely unbelievable and wonder *Does* he *even believe what he is saying?* The answer is probably yes. We have an incredible ability to deceive ourselves. Criminal psychologists speak about criminals who actually convince themselves that they didn't commit the crime. We all possess the ability to deceive ourselves, and we all engage that ability at different times and in varying degrees.

We do it sometimes out of convenience and sometimes out of cowardice. It is not necessarily that we are malicious; sometimes it is simply a survival technique. The truth seems so unbearable. But if we learn to listen to our bodies, if we learn to measure our inner comfort and discomfort, we quickly recognize the self-destructive element of deceit.

What are you not being honest with yourself about?

From honesty with self, we move to honesty with others. It is rare—if not impossible—to be more honest with another person than you are with yourself, so the more we harbor self-deception, the more deception will manifest in our communication with others. Sooner or later, everything within us manifests as an external reality.

Sometimes our self-deception stems simply from a lack of self-knowledge. When I ask people in my audiences to raise their hands if they think they are an above-average driver, more than eighty percent raise their hands. Raw mathematics suggests that a large number of those people are wrong. The other option is that my seminars attract only the best drivers, but that option seems unlikely. Are they lying to me? I don't think so. Are they consciously deceiving themselves? I doubt it. But a certain percentage of those people are probably still wrong, and regardless of their intent, the error is still impacting their lives and the lives of others. Perhaps when they are driving, they tell themselves that they can drive a little faster than most because they are better drivers than most. It is a small thing, a simple example, but it illustrates how important a searching self-knowledge is if we are striving to be honest with ourselves and with others.

Most people consider themselves to be honest people. Are you an honest person?

Try this: For the next week, carry with you a notebook and pen everywhere you go. Keep track of each time you find yourself telling a lie or thinking of telling a lie. In the latter cases, ask yourself, *If I weren't doing this exercise, would I have told the lie?* You will be amazed to realize how many times you are in situations in which you would ordinarily stretch the truth or tell a lie.

Doing this exercise will give you a heightened awareness of your thoughts and actions throughout the day. It also introduces an element of accountability; you will more than likely be more honest with yourself and with others. The exercises at the end of each chapter are designed to help you apply the lessons of enduring happiness to your life in this way. They help increase your awareness of the change you desire and create the accountability necessary to implement sustainable changes in your life.

The other side of honesty and integrity is when we don't speak up when we should. How easy it would have been for Jean Valjean in *Les Miserables* to hold his tongue at the trial of that poor fool, to let the stranger suffer for his crimes, allowing Valjean to conceal his true identity forever. But it would have been dishonest. Sometimes not to speak is to lie.

Virtue is not something you can switch on and off like a light. I don't know how many times someone has said to me over the years, "I was told this in confidence, but . . ." Immediately this person is telling me that I cannot tell them something in confidence. How often, when caught in a lie, people reply, "But I would never lie about that stuff to you!" Honesty is not a part-time virtue.

From honesty with self and honesty with others, we then move to honesty *about* others. How easy it is to fall into talking about other people and situations, with people whom we know or don't know and situations that we have little or no knowledge of. In a few short moments, we can cast a shadow over the character of a person who is not present to defend him- or herself. We can do irreparable damage to a person's reputation with just a few words.

Gossip is often at the core of our daily dishonesty. Willingly or unwillingly, consciously or unconsciously, when we talk about others, we are often participating in a spiraling episode of lies and deceit. Why do we do it? Usually not out of any malicious intent. More often than not, it's because we simply don't have the emotional energy to fight the battle or walk away or because we want to fit in and feel accepted or because we don't want to get on the wrong side of certain people. But all of this brings us to wonder how honest we are about other people. So let us ask ourselves three questions:

1. Am I honest with myself?
2. Am I honest with others?
3. Am I honest about others?

Sadly, many people feel that they need to lie and deceive to succeed in whatever they do. In many ways, because of the state of our social, political, and business systems, the discussion of honesty can often descend into a rather negative conversation. But before we move on from our brief discussion about honesty and truth, allow me to highlight one of the very positive aspects of this subject and one of the most attractive qualities a person can aspire to.

I have always had enormous respect for people who seek the truth. Are you a truth seeker? It is not an easy thing to be. Very often when we have questions about something in our lives, we don't actively seek the truth about that situation or issue; we just muddle along as these questions fester in our hearts and minds, making us restless and creating dis-ease. But as we grow wiser and decide to actively seek character through virtue, we become hungry for the truth. There are few qualities more attractive in a person than this truth seeking.

Do we seek the truth in our lives? Do we foster a love of truth in our hearts and minds? Do we celebrate truth? Or do we avoid truth when it comes to certain issues, because we have a sense that discovering the truth may challenge us to change the way we live our lives? It is in this dynamic, the seeking or avoiding of truth, that the great self-deception begins.

Integrity and honesty are not acquired simply by wishing for them, nor do all people gain them simply with the passing of time. To possess them and hold on to them, we must seek them proactively and guard them vigilantly. They are much more likely to be lost than they are to be found over time if we do not earnestly nurture them.

In many moments every day, we must choose between a radical honesty with self and others, and an honesty of convenience that sooner or later descends into a web of lies and deceit. At these crossroads we are choosing between our authentic self and some second-rate version of the amazing person we are capable of being.

Honesty and integrity are just two of the many virtues we can aspire to. I have used them here as an example because they hold a central place in the development of character and because they are prerequisites for many other virtues. The quest for character begins with honesty. There is no personal integrity without honesty, and there is no enduring happiness without personal integrity. It is time to take a personal inventory and assess the state of our character.

To attain real virtue is no easy task. It requires constant dedication to truth. Few people have enough ambition to want to be a man or woman of virtue today, and this is the first sign of decay in any civilization. I hope with all my heart that we can reawaken ambition for virtue in our own lives and in the lives of the people around us.

THE ENEMY OF CHARACTER

The enemy of character is ego. Within each of us there are two selves, a true self and a false self. The two selves are constantly battling with each other for supremacy. The true self speaks for character, and the false self speaks for ego. The authentic self finds its identity in all things that are good, true, beautiful, and noble, while the ego is constantly making demands based on insecurity and self-aggrandizement. Character is the emergence of the true self, while ego is the ugly head of the false self. Character is the ambassador of the higher self, while ego represents the lower self.

Which self will you choose? The higher self or the lower self? The authentic self or the false self? Character or ego? Are you willing to dismiss the constant demands of the ego and painstakingly build an identity of character one virtue at a time?

It is this conflict between the higher self and the lower self, between character and ego, which surrounds the whole human drama. All great music, movies, and stories are centered on this struggle. Within people and between people, within nations and between nations, the battle is between character and ego. All we are ever witnessing in human relations is this struggle between the higher self and the lower self. Character and ego are constantly vying for dominance within us, and the inner reality seeks an external expression.

Our egos place us at the center of the universe, and everyone and everything else is either in place, or out of place, according to our whims, cravings, fancies, and self-centered desires. When we are living from an ego-centered perspective, everything happens in relation to us. Everything we hear and see, we hear and see in relation to us. When people speak to us, we don't try to understand what they are trying to communicate; we filter what they are say-

ing and hear what they are saying only in relation to what is of interest to us or how it might affect us. An extreme example might be
that someone close to us gets very sick and we are upset because
their illness has interfered with our plans.

Life never happens as we think it will, and events rarely unfold
exactly as we would like them to, so when we are living from an
ego-centered point of view we are constantly frustrated and disappointed. Consumed by ego, everyone and everything seem to be
always out of place. But the world of ego is an illusion. The reality
is that everyone and everything is in place, exactly as they should
be in this very moment. We are out of place. By succumbing to the
mental seduction of the ego, we have erroneously placed ourselves
at the center of the universe, where we most certainly do not belong. Everything may seem out of place, but in fact it is we who are
out of place.

The more we submit to the demands of ego, the larger the ego
grows, and the more control we give to the ego, the more irritable,
restless, and frustrated we become. This is because things will inevitably not always turn out as we would like them to. There are so
many factors beyond our control, and when we don't get what we
want, the ego throws a tantrum, just as an undisciplined child
does. This child sees his or her desires as the number-one priority,
and when those desires are not fulfilled the world is wrong and the
universe is out of balance from his or her egotistical point of view.
We all fall into this behavior from time to time. We may be going
to meet someone and the other person is running late. In the
grand scheme of things, it's nothing, but we can make a huge deal
out of it. We may not even say anything to anyone, but inside we
allow it to grind away. How many men do I know who are always
complaining about how long it takes their wives to get ready? They
could just sit down and relax and read while they are waiting—
a few minutes here or there is not going to make that much of a

difference—but they choose to let it upset them. In these scenarios, and many more, the real issue is that events are not unfolding exactly as we want them to.

The truth is this: We are not the center of the universe, and when we try to place ourselves there, we set ourselves up for disappointment and frustration. The ego is never satisfied, whereas the authentic self is satisfied simply with embracing this moment as an opportunity to progress toward the-best-version-of-itself in any way it can. If waiting patiently will help you become a better person, the authentic self is satisfied with waiting patiently, but the ego will be restless. If helping someone else fulfill a dream will help you build a better relationship with that person, the authentic self wants to celebrate that, but the ego wants you to always be the center of attention. The authentic self is genuinely interested in other people, while the ego is interested only in what other people can do for it.

Character leads to enduring happiness. Living only through the ego leads to empty and fleeting pleasure. Invest in character, and it will see you through good times and bad. Invest in ego, and it is like building a home on quicksand.

Growing in Virtue

We live in a fix-it society. Turn on your television on any given day and just surf through the channels. One commercial after another, one infomercial after another, they are all offering to fix something. There is a fix for heartburn and a fix for obesity, a fix for sleeplessness, and a fix for diarrhea. There is a fix for runny noses, ugly noses, and stuffy noses. There is a fix for hair loss and a fix for pimples. There is a fix for debt and a fix for loneliness.

Psychiatrist Gerald May makes the observation that in all kinds of advertising, from the blatant affront of TV commercials to the subtleties of word-of-mouth, nothing can escape the fix. And it's not just that fixes are offered. The message also is that one "ought" to be fixed. That if perchance one should pass a certain fix by, not partake of its wondrous possibilities, one really isn't being very responsible for one's self.

There are two problems with all this fixing. First, some of the things that people are trying to fix about us, and that we are trying to fix about ourselves, are not broken. They are exactly as they are intended to be. Some of the imperfections that we are obsessed with changing are part of our perfection. Being perfectly yourself means being perfectly imperfect. And second, for everything else that doesn't fall into the first category, if you look a little more closely you will discover that we are just treating symptoms rather than actually fixing anything at all. If you have heartburn or cannot sleep at night, you should be asking yourself what it is about your lifestyle that is creating the problem.

Our lives genuinely improve only when we grow in virtue. Any other change is simply cosmetic. If we really want to improve ourselves, our lives, and our society, then we need to begin to switch the focus off of money, celebrity, and talent and onto character and virtue.

Growing in virtue is the work of our lives. Everything that happens, everything we do is just an opportunity to grow in virtue. When the person in front of you is fumbling through her purse to find the forty-nine cents for the cashier and you are beginning to get restless and frustrated, what's really happening? It's just an opportunity for you to grow in patience. Make virtue your goal, and you will find that the moments of the day come bearing the gift of opportunity.

But if we truly wish to grow in virtue, we must wean ourselves off of instant gratification. Not only do we live in a fix-it society but we also live in a quick-fix society. We overlook character and virtue because they are not quick fixes. Both require time and effort.

Growing in virtue is not easy. It requires real and constant effort. But the beauty of this effort is that if you grow in one virtue, you will automatically grow in every other virtue. If you decide to focus on becoming a more patient person, you will automatically become a kinder person. Kindness and patience are interconnected. It is easier for a patient person to be kind, just as it is easier for a patient person to be generous, because a patient person is not consumed with his or her own gratification. If you focus your efforts on becoming a more temperate person, you will automatically become a more just person. An honest person finds it easier to be patient and just. A patient person finds it easy to control his temper or practice moderation.

You may be wondering where you should begin. The answer is different for every person. You alone must decide. Just pick a virtue: honesty, patience, moderation, kindness, humility, courage, perseverance, compassion, hope, charity, generosity, wisdom, gentleness . . .   Pick a virtue and focus on developing that virtue in yourself. Write it down. Remind yourself each morning. Stop to reflect on your progress at intervals throughout the day and at the end of each day. Reflect on times when you have exercised the virtue and times when you should have but did not. As the days and weeks pass, you will be able to objectively say, "I am becoming a more generous person" or "I am becoming a more honest person." Then celebrate your progress.

Focus on one virtue for a couple of weeks, and then switch your focus to another virtue. One virtue at a time, you will begin to build a castle of character to live in.

In each moment of the day, just do the next right thing. When you feel yourself losing your temper, control it. When you recognize that you are getting impatient, breathe deeply and allow the moment to give you the gift of patience. When you encounter someone in need, be generous with your time, talents, or treasure. In each moment, just do the next right thing and your life will begin to flood with joy.

THERE ARE NO PERSONAL ACTS

If we reject the challenge to grow in virtue, we fall easily into a minimalism that manifests in the two great excuses. I have already mentioned "This is who I am!" We often make this excuse not in celebration of our authentic self but in defense of a substitute lazy and defeated self. The second of the great excuses that we use to justify our self-destructive behavior is "I am not hurting anybody!"

One of the governing principles of the universe is connection. Everything in creation is connected. When we pollute and scar the earth by emitting toxins and rape the land of her natural resources, the earth responds with rising water levels, earthquakes, hurricanes, and harmful ozone rays. The earth is not retaliating; it is simply trying to heal itself.

Similar connections exist between people. To believe that what we do in our hometown does not affect people at the other end of the country or the other end of the world is the naïveté, ignorance, and self-centeredness of the modern era. There are no personal acts. Everything we do affects the people around us. Everything we do affects all people, sooner or later. The sum of all human action is passed down through history.

In times past, when humankind lived more in tune with nature, when we were tied to the earth, we understood this with great clarity. In those times, we understood very clearly that if we polluted the water supply upstream, the people downsteam would be endangered. Today, the rivers are not so easy to see and recognize.

We buy our water in bottles, believing that there will always be clean water for us to drink. In politics and business, in relationships and the arts, when we pollute the water upstream, the people downstream suffer.

Just because you do something in the privacy of your home, behind closed doors, with no one else involved and no one else to witness the act, does not mean that that act does not affect other people. Every human act affects the future of humanity. Your actions, however private, have consequences for you and for all of humanity. Your actions profoundly affect your inner reality, and sooner or later your inner reality will seek an outer expression through your words and actions or your silence and inaction.

The way of the universe is connection. In ways we will perhaps never understand, we are all connected. Too often we think of ourselves as different or set apart or independent. Sometimes these are just words and illusions. We are much more alike than we are different. We are so much more together than we are apart, and infinitely more interdependent than we are independent. When we hurt ourselves, we hurt everyone. "I'm not hurting anyone!" is just another attempt to avoid personal responsibility in a world where everything we think, do, and say affects someone, somewhere, sooner or later.

PUT CHARACTER FIRST

> Good character is that quality which makes one dependable whether being watched or not, which makes one truthful when it is to one's advantage to be a little less than truthful, which makes one courageous when faced with great obstacles, which endows one with the firmness of wise self-discipline.
>
> —ARTHUR ADAMS

The third lesson for enduring happiness is this:

PUT CHARACTER FIRST.

In every moment of the day we must train ourselves to put character ahead of financial gain and professional advancement, to value character more than momentary pleasures and the esteem of other people, and to place character ahead of our own designs and desires. Putting character first means that we will allow our thoughts, decisions, actions, and relationships to become subordinate to this quest to become and remain authentic.

Character is the greatest investment any of us can make. Begin to invest in yourself. Investing requires discipline, self-control, and patience. Many of us lack one or all of these qualities. Think of it in the financial sense. If you saved one dollar a day from the age of twenty-two until the age of sixty-five and invested that money at an average return of seven percent, you would retire with close to four hundred thousand dollars. Three dollars a day would give you a million dollars, and yet, most people retire with little or no net worth. Is it because they couldn't afford to set aside one, two, or three dollars a day, or is it because they lacked the discipline, self-control, and patience?

Very simply put, we live in a spending-centered society. Spending reflects ego, and character reflects saving. Most people save less than one percent of their annual income. Worse than that, millions spend more each year than they earn. Invest in yourself. Start to build a dynamic portfolio of virtues. Add all the great virtues to your character portfolio and watch your future blossom. Money and possessions have their appeal, rapidly advancing careers can fuel our egos, and pleasure can be ever so seductive, but character is what will see you through good times and bad. Make character your number-one priority in every sphere of your life. Put character first.

Applying the Third Lesson for
Enduring Happiness:

PUT CHARACTER FIRST

I will apply the third lesson of enduring happiness
to my life by taking the following steps:

1. I will put character first by making an investment in character. In my daily life, I will start to see every situation as an opportunity to grow in character by developing a variety of virtues. I will focus on one virtue at a time, knowing that by growing in one virtue I will necessarily increase my capacity for other virtues. Once I can honestly say that I have progressed in this virtue and established it as a habit, I will choose another virtue to focus on. I will look for patience, kindness, humility, gentleness, forgiveness, honesty, integrity, and love in myself and in others. I will seize every chance to celebrate these and other virtues.

2. I will pursue rigorous honesty with myself and with others. From time to time, I will pause to reflect on the following questions: Am I honest with myself? Am I honest with others? Am I honest about others? I will be mindful never to put someone else in a situation where they may have to be anything but completely honest.

3. I will proactively nurture positive habits in each of the four areas of life: physical, emotional, intellectual, and spiritual. I will be mindful of myself as a whole person and will approach others conscious of the many aspects we are all seeking to balance.

4. I will resist the constant demands of ego by listening more attentively to the voice of my true self. Each day I will try to be increasingly attentive to what is driving me—the insecurity of ego or the integrity of character. I will move beyond our culture's constant concern for appearances and center myself on a concern for character.

Four

86,400 Hours

I f you graduated from high school at the age of eighteen, went to college and graduated in four years, then went out into the real world and got a real job working forty hours a week and worked forty-eight weeks a year, took four weeks' annual vacation (two weeks more than most people), and retired at the age of sixty-five, you will have worked 86,400 hours by the time you retire.

Each year I visit more than a hundred U.S. cities, and most afternoons before my main presentation, I visit a high school. I believe it is important to give young people a life-directing message at that age, so that they won't need a life-changing message when they are thirty, forty, fifty, or older. I speak to them about how important it is to find something they can be passionate about and dedicate the professional aspect of their life to.

Work is not everything, but when you are doing work that doesn't engage you or, worse yet, work that you despise, it can massively affect every other aspect of your life. It is simply impossible to create enduring happiness without finding an approach to work that allows you to thrive. Ideally this means finding work that you are passionate about, but even if you are not in your dream job—or don't know what your dream job would be—there are ways to thrive at work.

In explaining the 86,400-hour equation to high school students, I then ask them if they have any boring classes at school. They inevitably erupt. Of course they have a boring class at school. They are, after all, teenagers. So I ask them how long a class lasts. Students call out from their seats, "Fifty minutes" or "An hour" or "Ninety minutes," depending on that particular school's timetable. "And how slowly does time pass when you are in the middle of that boring class?" I ask. Again they erupt and moan. "How long does it feel like?" I ask. "Forever," they cry back.

Standing there in silence, I let them simmer down a little, and then I say, "Now I want you to immerse yourself in that experience of a boring class for a moment. Then I want you to multiply that by infinity and take it to the depths of eternity, and you will still have barely a glimpse of what is in store for you unless you think about, and I mean really think about, what you want to do with your 86,400 hours."

Thoreau was right. Most men and women lead lives of quiet desperation. But it isn't as though people sit around when they are in high school and think to themselves, *I really hope I can lead a life of quiet desperation when I grow up. Maybe I should stop by the guidance counselor and see if he can put together a really great plan for me to lead a life of quiet desperation.* No, people simply fail to plan, and as Napoleon observed, "Those that fail to plan can plan to fail."

Workplace Trends

Several months ago, I had the opportunity to conduct job interviews for a number of new positions at my organization. In all, I conducted almost fifty interviews with candidates who had been pulled from literally hundreds and hundreds of applicants. I was overwhelmed by the number of people who applied and the quality of the applicants. Every single one of them was already in what I thought was a really good job. In many cases, the candidates would be required to take pay cuts to move from high-paying corporate jobs into the nonprofit sector, but that didn't seem to phase them at all.

So I asked them all many questions, but their answers to one question in particular seemed to have a common theme. I asked each candidate, "You seem to have a great job at the moment. Why do you want to leave?" Forty-eight of the fifty candidates replied that they wanted to do something more meaningful with their lives, or with some variation of the same idea. I believe this reflects the greatest shift in the workplace of the twenty-first century and will affect corporate America more than anything else in the next fifty years. People want meaningful work.

In the 1980s, cash was king, and people seemed willing to work a hundred hours a week as long as you paid them more money. The 1980s were all about money and possessions. In the 1990s, there was a significant and noticeable shift in attitude away from an overwhelming emphasis on financial compensation and toward a desire for leisure. A growing number of people began to say, "I don't care how much money you pay me—I am just not willing to work more hours. I don't want more money as much as I want more freedom with my schedule, more leisure time."

Another factor is that throughout this entire period, the corporate world has changed considerably, particularly when it comes to loyalty. Many people who were laid off came to a frightening realization about how little control they had over their destinies in the corporate schema and, more strikingly, how little their efforts were appreciated. For a whole variety of reasons, people have started to take their lives back, emphasizing independence, family life, leisure, and health and well-being.

The money focus of the 1980s evolved into the leisure focus of the 1990s, and now there is a new trend emerging. People certainly still want to be financially compensated and they want to have time to spend with family and friends, but above all else, they yearn for meaningful work. And they are willing to sacrifice some of the money and leisure to have it. This shift in workplace attitude is only going to gather more and more momentum as people continue to awaken to their need to be engaged more passionately at work.

FULFILLMENT @ WORK

Theodore Roosevelt said this about work: "The best prize life offers is the chance to work hard at work worth doing." I don't agree with him entirely. I think that dynamic relationships are probably the best that life has to offer, and I suspect that having children and grandchildren probably rank somewhere near the top of the list also. But I do agree that one of the best things in this life is the chance to work hard at something that is actually worth doing.

When I reminisce about my time in high school and the friends I made during those years, I am always amazed at how so few people end up doing what they thought they would do when they were in high school. Most people seem to find their way, but very few do exactly what they imagined they would do when they were in high school.

If you had told me while I was in high school that I would become a successful author and speaker, the idea would have seemed nothing more than absurd to me. Luke, one of my best friends from high school, often reminds me of an incident that took place in my English class during my senior year. Our teacher, Mrs. Grace, was handing back our latest papers, reflections on *The Heart of Darkness*, I believe. For some reason, I was never able to find my way into the good graces of that teacher. I had tried hard in the class, and for the first time in my life I was struggling—hopelessly, it seemed—to get a good grade. Nothing I did was ever good enough in that class. Mrs. Grace walked around the classroom handing out papers. She dropped mine on my desk, and I discovered that she had awarded me a grade of one out of a possible twenty. This seemed like the final straw. Surely putting your name on the paper and demonstrating that you had actually read the book, both of which I had done, was worthy of at least five, maybe even six. But no, apparently not. Luke reminds me that I screwed the paper up into a ball and threw it over my teacher's head and into the trashcan in the corner of the classroom. My classmates roared. Yes, if you had told me in high school that I would become a writer, I would have just laughed.

Today I spend my life speaking and writing. What an enormous privilege! I never lose sight of that. I am constantly in awe of the life I am living. Day after day, people seek me out to ask my counsel on any number of issues, but after relationships, the most common struggle in people's lives today is with their work. They don't feel appreciated. They don't feel that they are living in their genius. They feel that they are wasting their lives and that they could be doing so much more. They feel that their creativity is not being tapped, and they yearn to make a more meaningful contribution. The world is full of people who are miserable at work.

I love speaking and I love writing. The speaking comes much

more naturally to me than the writing, but I love both, and they seem to feed off of each other in a rather dynamic way. Is everything about my work life perfect? Of course it isn't. There are a lot of hotels and airports, it's always a hassle to find a good meal, something or someone is always running late, and the glamour of travel wears off very quickly. There are a lot of wake-up calls at 3:30 AM, and on those days it often takes me a little longer to grow into an attitude of gratitude about my life. A couple of weeks ago, I was at home and had decided to sleep in a little. I was lying there in bed semiconscious, and the phone rang. I picked it up, said, "Thank you," and hung up. A minute or so later, the phone rang again. My mother said, "Why did you hang up on me?" I had forgotten I was at home and thought her first call was my wake-up call.

But I love my life and I would never trade it for anyone else's. I have found something I am passionate about. I get to do what I love and for that I am so grateful. I never wake up and think, *Oh, I have to go to work today!* In fact, I very rarely think of what I do as work, but I suspect that the people who surround me would probably tell you that I work harder than anyone they know.

We all spend too much time working not to be able to experience a deep sense of satisfaction from our work. Fulfillment at work and enduring happiness are inseparably linked.

The words of Lin Yu-t'ang, a writer, translator, and editor, lend a powerful perspective to our reflection at this point:

So much unhappiness, it seems to me, is due to nerves; and bad nerves are the result of having nothing to do, or doing a thing badly, unsuccessfully, or incompetently. Of all the unhappy people in the world, the unhappiest are those who have not found something they want to do. True happiness comes to him who does his work well, followed by a relaxing and refreshing period of rest. True happiness comes from the right amount of work for the day.

Let us endeavor to find the right work and then seek to do the right amount of that work each day.

The Meaning of Work

So why do we work? What is the meaning of work? What value is work designed to bring to our lives? For the most part, the idea of work carries negative connotations in our society. Most people don't like their work and they don't like to work. So when someone says things such as "Great relationships require work," they have a negative reaction. The first problem is that many of us are engaged in work that does not stimulate or engage us, and the second problem is that given the choice, many people would sit around idle and waste their lives completely. That's a sweeping statement, but if you think it isn't true, conduct a brief study on how many people you know who already spend the time that they have doing whatever they wish with it.

We encourage children to work hard because whether we are able to articulate it or not, we know that working hard and happiness are linked. I was giving a presentation to a corporate group recently, and during one of the question-and-answer sessions, one of the attendees offhandedly commented that if Adam and Eve hadn't eaten the apple, we would never have had to work. That's a common misconception. But in fact, as I pointed out to him in the Judeo-Christian scriptures to which he was referring, even before the apple was eaten, God had placed Adam in the garden to "tend and till the soil."

Work is not a punishment. What is the meaning of work? Why do we go to work? Some would argue, "Because we have to!" and others would say, "To make money." But both would be wrong. In truth, you don't have to do anything. Nobody can make you do anything. At some level, we choose to go to work. And contrary to the overwhelmingly popular view that we work to make money, making money is actually the secondary purpose for work.

The primary meaning, purpose, and value of work is that when we work hard and well, when we pay attention to the details of our work, we develop character and virtue. By working hard, I develop the virtues of perseverance and fortitude; by paying attention to the details of my work, I develop patience and responsibility; and by working well, I develop diligence.

When work is approached in the right way and with the right frame of mind, it helps us to become more perfectly ourselves. Who you are is infinitely more important than what you do or what you have. Like everything else in this life, the value of work is in the way it helps us to become the-best-versions-of-ourselves.

Work is at the essence of our quest for character. It is important that we remain active. Work is a source of a healthy mind and body. In ancient civilizations, retirement was always a punishment. More than 2,350 years ago, Aristotle pointed out that happiness resides in activity, both mental and physical, and not idleness. Happiness is found in doing things that we can take pride in doing well and hence can enjoy doing. One of the errors of our culture's pursuit of happiness is that we identify enjoyment with mere amusement and doing nothing. We tend to confuse happiness with mere relaxation and being entertained.

If we wish to discover our authentic selves, few things will be more helpful to us than hard work. Too often we make the mistake of turning to idleness to discover who we truly are. How often people say to me, "I just need a couple of months off to work this out" or "If only I could get away from all this, I would be able to get my head straight." These are things we tell ourselves, and in doing so we convince ourselves that we cannot work out our dilemmas where we are right now. Getting away is usually not the answer. I won't say that it is never the answer, because sometimes it is. But it is rarely less pressure and usually more pressure that brings the answers we seek. In architecture, if you wish to strengthen an arch that has become weak, you increase the load on the arch. It goes against our natural instincts, perhaps, but an increase in the load joins the loose parts of the arch together more firmly. Our natural inclination is to remove the weight carried by the arch, but to do so would be a mistake. The same is often true in our lives.

Working halfheartedly may reap you the same financial compensation as working with all your heart and soul, but it will slowly begin to rot your heart and mind and soul. Humans were not designed for halfheartedness. So often I have heard people talk about how they will get back at their boss by being lazy or dragging their feet on a project. This is like drinking poison and expecting the other person to die.

Thousands of men and women go to work every day to jobs that they are not crazy about simply to support their families financially. There is nothing wrong with this. In and of itself, it is good and noble. If the only meaning they ever find in their work is building character and supporting their family's financial needs, they would be doing a good and noble thing. But at the same time, I think we have a responsibility as a society to try to move all people toward more fulfilling work, work that engages their unique gifts and abilities.

The meaning of work is not to make money or to be fun or entertaining. If we make money and enjoy our work, that's all the better, but the primary meaning of work is to help us to develop character and virtue. So wherever you are, whatever your work is at this time in your life, give it your all. Collecting the trash has an infinite value if it is done well with the goal of growing in character and virtue. It may not be considered the most meaningful work, but we can bring meaning to it by seeing it not as an end in itself but as a means to building character. If it is a man's job to collect the trash and he does it well, works hard, and pays attention to the details of his work, with every passing hour he will become a-better-version-of-himself. From this perspective, all honest work has an intrinsic value. Work is an opportunity not just to make money but also to invest in ourselves.

Two Fables

Stories have a way of cutting through the clutter of our minds and the prejudices of our hearts and leading us to new discoveries about ourselves, our world, and the road before us. When we were children, my parents use to read Aesop's fables to my brothers and me. Allow me to share two of Aesop's brief fables with you that have particular relevance to our conversation.

The first is "Hercules and the Wagoner."

A wagoner was driving his team along a muddy lane with a full load behind them, when the wheels of his wagon sank so deep in the mire that no efforts of his horses could move them. As he stood there, looking helplessly on and calling loudly at intervals upon Hercules for assistance, the god himself appeared and said to him, "Put your shoulder to the wheel, man, and goad your horses, and then you may call on Hercules to assist you. If you won't lift a finger to help yourself, you can't expect Hercules or anyone else to come to your aid."

Make the first move. Take the first step. Now is your time. The whole universe conspires to assist those who pursue their dreams. If what you desire is meaningful work that you can throw yourself into passionately each day, step toward it. You cannot expect it to chase you down; you must chase it down.

The second fable is "The Farmer and His Sons."

A farmer, being at death's door and desiring to impart to his sons a secret of much moment, called them round him and said, "My sons, I am shortly about to die. I would have you know, therefore, that in my vineyard there lies a hidden treasure. Dig, and you will find it." As soon as their father was dead, the sons took spade and fork and turned up the soil of the vineyard over and over again, in their search for the treasure which they supposed to lie buried there. They found none, however, but the vines, after so thorough a digging, produced a crop such as had never before been seen.

The toil and the treasure are linked. But it is not enough simply to work hard, nor is it enough only to pray. You must work hard at the right things, and pray hard for the right things. It is also important to recognize that the treasure is not always financial, and that the satisfaction of doing something worthy with your life is worth more than a mountain of gold.

Find something that you consider worthy of your talent and character, and give yourself to it. Only then will you experience the joy of work. Not that it is easier. In many ways, it can be harder than ever before, because as you become more fully invested, your standards will rise.

FINDING YOUR PASSION

There may be ways to bring meaning to work, and work may offer an intrinsic opportunity to grow in character and virtue, but none of that is to say that you should not enjoy your work or find something to do with your 86,400 hours that you find fulfilling and meaningful. But finding something that you can be passionate about and meeting the demands of the economic reality of our modern culture is becoming increasingly more difficult.

If you could do anything, what would you do? Are you willing to make sacrifices in order to do it? Are you willing to give up money or status, downsize to a smaller home, or give up free time for more training or schooling?

I have always asked that first question when conducting job interviews. The candidates are often afraid to tell you because they are concerned that they will sound as if they don't want the job they are interviewing for. The truth is, you want them to be honest. You are trying to learn a little about what they aspire to. You can tell a lot about a person by what he or she aspires to.

The first step, of course, is to work out what your passions are. Most people don't really know. They know what they don't want because they already have it or have seen it. But few people really know what they want. Even fewer have a clear sense of what they are well suited to.

What are your passions? Take a few minutes and make a list. Just write from your stream of consciousness. Don't overthink things. You may be passionate about chocolate, baseball, or educating people about what is causing the massive increase in cancer. Write them down. Write it all down, anything that excites you, anything that energizes you. Just write it all down.

When we are children, people ask us all the time, "What are

you going to be when you grow up?" But it seems today, more and more adults are asking themselves, *What am I going to be when I grow up?*

In an e-mail a couple of weeks ago, one of my readers wrote, "Today I caught myself counting the days to the weekend—and it is only Monday!" Is the fact that so many people wish five days away in order to get to two not a clear indication that today's workers are chronically dissatisfied?

Whenever I talk to people on planes or at book signings, I like to observe their rising and falling levels of energy and enthusiasm as we discuss a variety of topics. When most people talk about their work, they use a completely different tone from the one they use in talking about their children or their next vacation. In another e-mail, one of my readers explained, "Today is my third day back at work since my annual two-week vacation and I am already planning next year's. I have to believe that if I was more satisfied in my work I would spend less time planning and daydreaming about my next vacation." Others speak about rewarding themselves just to get through the days and weeks. Some people reward themselves with chocolate, others by going shopping or by taking themselves out to a favorite restaurant for dinner, and others by drinking or vegetating in front of the television for hours every night. If we were more passionately engaged in our work, would all of these rewards play such a prominent role in our lives? I think not.

So what are you going to do when you grow up? It's not like it is as it was a hundred years ago, when a man did what his father did and a woman had babies and took care of the house. Today the possibilities are extraordinary. The bigger problem today is probably that there are just too many options. I am not going to tell you that you can do anything you set your mind to; that would be a lie. But I am going to tell you that you deserve to have work that engages you passionately. I am not going to tell you that someone is just going to walk along and give you such a job. It is most likely going to be very hard to move from where you are to where you would like to be. The secret is finding something that you are well suited for.

The next question is this: How will you know when you have found your passion? When we are exercising our talents and abilities in a role that we are passionate about, we experience timelessness. When I get done speaking to an audience for an hour, it seems as if it were just five minutes. I sit down in my study to write, and the next thing I know, three hours have passed, but to me it feels like I just sat down fifteen minutes earlier. When we live in our genius, time passes almost without notice. I want you to experience this timelessness. Remember the high school students I was speaking with? Consider two classes in high school, one that you loved and the other that you hated. The class you loved passed you by in a flash and the class you hated seemed to drag on forever. The class you loved represents living in your passion, and the class you hated represents quiet desperation.

Do we always experience this timelessness? No. Sometimes I sit here at my computer and the time just seems to drag or I can't stop thinking about somewhere I would rather be. The timelessness isn't always there, but we live for the times that it is. And once you have experienced it, there is no mistaking it for anything else.

Not everyone must work in a corporate situation to find happiness. Though it may seem a little old-fashioned to some, many of the happiest women I know find their passionate work in raising their children and tending the home. There are a great many men and women who are retired who are engaged in volunteer work that they are more passionate about than they ever were about their careers. And the nonprofit world is becoming more and more attractive to people looking for meaningful work that they can passionately immerse themselves in.

People ask me all the time why my foundation's sole focus for its charitable work is with schools and colleges. The reasons are many, but one is because when I was young, nobody ever told me to find something that I loved doing and give my life to it. All the focus was on getting to the next level, learning new things, reading more textbooks, completing assignments, passing exams, developing more useful skills, and moving on to the new level. Strange, isn't it, that nobody ever sat me down and said, "Matthew, if you could do anything with your life, what would you do?" or "Matthew, what are you really passionate about?" or "Matthew, what do you think you would be really good at and would enjoy?" or "Matthew, what do you feel you could do with your life that could really make a contribution?"

For all the resources our society pours into education, we so often miss the really important questions. We can't see the forest for the trees. We graduate with the answers to so many questions, but have we asked the right questions? Surely asking the right questions is more important than having all of the answers to all of the wrong questions.

Not a day goes by that I am not grateful for the gift of meaningful work. I have work that I can throw myself into with passion, energy, and enthusiasm, and I am infinitely aware of how rare that is. I have found it, but most people don't, and that is one of the great untreated tragedies of our culture. Each night after my seminars, I sit at a table and sign books. My friends sometimes ask me why I sit there and sign all those books. It is a small way of thanking people for giving me a chance to work hard at something that is actually worth doing.

With all my heart, I hope that you will find your way toward an opportunity to work hard at something that is actually worth doing, and that you will encourage your children, spouse, and friends to do the same. Think about it. How many people do you know who are truly happy in their work? How many people do you know who are in a role that is genuinely a good fit for them?

BABY STEPS

It's time to find something you can do and do passionately. Don't delay. Do something today to move in the direction of an occupation or position about which you are more passionate. It may take five years before you are in a role that engages you in the way you yearn to be engaged, but if you don't start today, it will take five years and one day.

I remember the excitement I felt as a child my first day of school or the night before a big game, summer vacation, my birthday, or Christmas. As an adult I am learning to rediscover that excitement, not about the same things, but about things new and different. Why does that excitement fade for so many of us? I'm not sure I know. Maybe we just become jaded by experience and disappointment. Perhaps we just get preoccupied with all the practical details of life and lose our capacity for such excitement. Or is it fear? Do we become afraid of new challenges and experiences and the change they bring with them? That's not to say that we didn't have fear in our childhood. We did, but we also had the courage to step up and step out, the inner drive to go out on a limb, to experience new horizons, or we had others around to gently or not so gently push us forward. I remember how scared I was when my father took the training wheels off my bike for the first time, and I remember the pain and shame of then falling off my bike a couple of times in front of my brothers and friends as I got the knack of riding without the training wheels. But I can also remember the thrill and exhilaration of riding down the street on my bike without the training wheels . . . my first taste of this kind of freedom. I can also remember the stomach-churning, heart-thumping fear of my first kiss, but survived that too. You have your own experiences and examples. Remember them. Our past can give us courage for the future or instill fear of the future; the choice is ours. We choose what we focus on when we look back.

It is time now, once again, to take the training wheels off. It is time now for the courage of a first kiss. It is time now for the excitement and giddiness of childhood. Do you remember how far away your birthday seemed as a child when you still had to wait another week? Time is an illusion. Do your dreams seem far away from you now? Time is just an illusion.

Several years ago I met a young man and his wife in Pennsylvania. At the time, Ray asked if he could have some time to speak to me privately about something he was struggling with personally. He explained, as so many do, that he was unfulfilled in his work and that he had felt a growing restlessness to follow his dreams since he read *The Rhythm of Life*.

I asked him some searching questions to get a sense of his situation, and he explained that he worked for a custom clothing company that his family owned but really wanted to move into the area of personal fitness. Further delving revealed the feelings of obligation, inner conflict, and fear of guilt that so often accompany situations involving family businesses. We then discussed the security that his current job provided and his wife's hesitation about his following his dream.

People like Ray come to me every week, but I have never seen anyone handle the transition with the patience and discipline I saw him handle it. "What's the dream?" I asked him. "If you could do anything, what would that look like?" He explained that owning his own health and fitness center was his dream.

"What's the first step?" I then asked. We talked about different options, and I encouraged him to do what I encourage everyone to do: Break it down into baby steps. Take the steps that don't require you to quit your current position first. Do what you can do on the side, after hours, in the evenings, and on weekends.

For Ray the first step was to get himself trained and licensed as a personal trainer. The next step was to start working as a personal trainer outside of his normal business hours. Many people take the first couple of steps and realize that it's not really what they thought it would be. If they quit their job just to take these interim steps, they are now in limbo. But as Ray made each step, his passion for personal fitness and health and well-being was ignited more and more.

It was probably twelve or eighteen months later that Ray sought me out again to discuss making the leap toward his dream. He wanted to open a gym. I must admit that at first I was hesitant. For a young man like him with a wife and two wonderful children, the financial risk of opening a full-service business in an industry dominated by chains made me a little nervous. But as he explained his plan, I began to think about the way he had already handled the transitional steps toward his dream. I thought to myself, *Character is destiny,* but I was still more than a little nervous for him.

One day I was going through my mail, and I found that he had sent me photos of the grand opening. But about a year later, he sent me one of the best letters I have ever received, explaining that his business was thriving, he was living his dream, that he had never felt more alive, and that if he had never read *The Rhythm of Life* he would still be printing T-shirts while trying to figure out what was missing in his life. Ray's story is one I bring to mind whenever I get discouraged.

So what are your baby steps? What are the interim steps between your current life and your dream that you can take without turning your life on its head? Maybe the first step is taking some time in silence and solitude to work out what you are most passionate about. Perhaps you need this time to identify the other interim steps. Then start to take those steps. Put together a current résumé. Enroll in a class. Start to research your area of interest. Seek out a mentor in that industry. Volunteer one day a month. Apply for a new job.

There are dozens of things you can do right now that will move you closer to work that is more fulfilling. Start doing some of them today. Make a commitment to yourself that in the next twenty-four hours you will do something to take a step in the direction of work that is better suited for you. One thing. Identify it and do it. Then, for the next ninety days, do one thing each day that will move you closer to or prepare you for your ideal job. Just by taking these small steps in the right direction you will begin to feel passion, energy, and enthusiasm flow back into your life, and these will give fuel to a gathering momentum. You will be amazed what can be accomplished in ninety days. Mark your calendar.

The fourth lesson for enduring happiness is this:

FIND WHAT YOU LOVE AND DO IT.

It may take months or years to find what you love. It make take months or years more to get yourself in a position where you can do what you love full time, but in some ways large or small, you can start doing what you love today. You may not be paid or recognized for it. That's okay. Once you engage in what you love doing, even if it is just for one hour a day, you will release an enormous amount of passion and energy into your life. Every area of your life will improve because you rediscover your enthusiasm for life.

Life is about love. What do you love doing? Do it. What do you love being? Be it. What do you love having? Have it and share it. Who do you love loving? Love them.

For many people, the only obstacle between them and work they can feel passionate about is financial commitments. It's another reason why I spend so much time with young people in high schools and colleges trying to help them work out what they are passionate about before they make all their life choices and commitments. This is something that is best worked out when we are young, single, and uncommitted.

If financial commitments are your only obstacle, then you have to return to our earlier questions. Are you willing to adjust your lifestyle? Do you value work you can be passionate about more than big-screen TVs and overpriced running shoes? Are you willing to make sacrifices? Is your family willing to make sacrifices? Would you live in a smaller house if you could go to work and love your work ninety percent of the time?

The other possibility to consider is that you may not be able to do what you love full time. It may not pay the bills at all. If that is the case, I encourage you to create a space in your life for the things you are passionate about. Engage your passions through your hobbies, by starting a small business on the side, or by working as a volunteer. One way or another, whether it is for forty hours a week or three hours a week, find what you love and do it.

FIND WHAT YOU LOVE AND DO IT

*I will apply the fourth lesson of enduring happiness
to my life by taking the following steps:*

1. I will work hard and well, paying attention to the details of my work—even if my work is menial or less meaningful than I would like it to be. I will bring meaning to my present work by consciously acknowledging that each hour of work, each task, is an opportunity to grow in virtue and character and become a-better-version-of-myself.

2. I will begin to identify and root out all half-heartedness in my life. If there are things that I cannot put my whole self into, I will examine them to determine their role or necessity in my life. If I can be rid of these things without harming others, or myself, and without abandoning a commitment I feel bound to hold, I will rid these things from my life at the earliest possible time. If I cannot in good faith walk away from these things for any valid reason, I will endure the despair of half-heartedness courageously.

3. I will make a list of all the things I am passionate about. In making the list I will not edit myself or restrict myself in any way whatsoever. I will write from my stream of consciousness, being careful not to overthink anything and writing down even the things that I think are completely impossible. I will celebrate the things I am passionate about in whatever ways I can, however small, here and now.

4. If I am not happy in my work, I will ask myself what the cause of this unhappiness is. Is it self, attitude, boss, coworkers, compensation, environment, or the very nature of the work itself? If I determine that it is best for me to move on, I will begin to act on that immediately but prudently. In the meantime, I will see the current situation as an opportunity to grow in patience and fortitude.

5. If I decide that it is time for me to find work that I can be more passionate about, I will proactively set about to do one thing in the next twenty-four hours that will lead me a step closer to work that is better suited for me and that I can energetically immerse myself in. And for the next ninety days, I will do one thing every day, however small, to prepare myself in some way for my new position.

6. I will pause occasionally and remember the different times in the past when I was afraid but was able to overcome my fear and step beyond the old boundaries—my first kiss, the first time I rode a bike without training wheels, my first roller coaster ride, my first swimming lesson. I will draw on these experiences to increase my courage when I encounter a moment of fear. I will not allow myself to be paralyzed by fear. I will remind myself that the measure of my life will be the measure of my courage, and I will step forth courageously.

Five

What Do You Believe?

We all believe in something. Even those of us who don't believe in something believe that they don't believe. An atheist *believes* that there is no God. Disbelief is not the absence of belief, but the presence of an opposing belief. An agnostic *believes* that he does not know if there is a God. The object of our beliefs may vary significantly, but we all believe. We cannot help but believe. It is impossible for us not to believe. It is part of who we are. The ability to believe is part of what makes us human. You cannot choose to believe or not to believe; you can only choose *what* you believe.

Our lives are directed by belief. You cross the street and you believe that the people driving cars from the other direction will stop at the red light. When you are driving, you have faith that the drivers coming from the other direction will stay on the other side of the road. You may not have complete faith in this, but you believe it to some extent. Without belief, we would be so paralyzed by fear of everyone and everything that we would be reduced to a mass of paranoia and would simply be unable to function in the world.

We all believe in something.

In this chapter it is not my goal to explore religious belief, which is what most people probably think about when the words *belief* and *faith* are mentioned. What I want to explore here is the personal and practical beliefs that affect our everyday lives. Do you believe it is better to just go out selfishly and get what you want, or do you believe that sharing adds value to your own life? Do you believe that you have a role in making the world a more harmonious place, or do you believe that world peace is completely beyond your control? Do you believe that people are intrinsically good, or do you believe that people will use you and wrong you if they are given the opportunity?

For many people these personal and practical beliefs are heavily influenced by their religious beliefs. But we all have the practical beliefs, even if we do not all have religious beliefs, and it is that common denominator that I wish to explore.

I find that what people do and what people say is interesting, but *why* people do what they do and say what they say is absolutely fascinating. This why is at the heart of intimacy and relationship. For example, if someone expresses a belief, our conditioned response in our hypercritical society is to judge that person according to how his or her belief differs from our own. This is an act of immaturity and insecurity, and ultimately an act of fear. As we grow in maturity, we become aware of two important realizations. The first is that people are not born with beliefs and opinions; these are the result of education and experience. Therefore people's beliefs and opinions are constantly being refined as they are exposed to new experiences and ongoing education.

The second is that belief is something that evolves in our lives. Have you always believed exactly what you believe today? Of course you haven't. You have developed your beliefs in response to the education and experiences that you have been exposed to along the way. And there is a very good chance that your beliefs will continue to change as you grow in intellectual and spiritual maturity in the years to come.

We all have the capacity to believe, and what we believe affects the way we live our lives. We are not born with beliefs. They are developed along the way. Taken on and discarded. Lived and tested. Abandoned and betrayed. Belief is at the essence of being human, so we cannot earnestly seek to become perfectly ourselves and ignore the role belief plays in our lives.

BEYOND THE DIVIDED LIFE

Why are beliefs so central to our discussion? The reason is because there is no faster way to create enduring unhappiness than to act against your beliefs. When we act contrary to our beliefs we create unhappiness for ourselves and for others. You cannot be perfectly yourself by betraying yourself. Beliefs play an enormous role in our happiness and unhappiness. The dilemma we face is in working out which of our beliefs are conditioned or based on erroneous education and which are good and true in and of themselves.

Wrestling with our beliefs is part of the process of maturity. Some of us cast off conditioned beliefs easily—too easily—while others have a really hard time divesting themselves even of self-destructive beliefs. In the past the belief that the man should be the provider for the family was almost universally held. Today we live in different times, and in many cases women are the sole providers for their families. Still, there are men who feel torn between a conditioned belief and the reality of their lives.

My father was raised in poverty in London. Later in his life, he was averse to risk when it came to investment. Over the years as he progressed from poverty to relative prosperity, his beliefs about money didn't change. He worried about money and that affected his ability to enjoy whatever money he had. His beliefs about money affected his happiness. These are simple examples, but whatever our beliefs, they influence our everyday lives. Sometimes we have beliefs that we are not even aware of because they are so deeply ingrained in us by past experiences.

Do you ever feel divided? Are you ever aware of your own inner conflicts? Do you feel drawn in two different directions? Just last year it seemed that every time one of my close friends asked me how I was feeling, my answer was "Conflicted!" My brother had just been killed tragically in a car accident, my father had died eighteen months earlier of cancer, and I was questioning many things in my life and in our world. I just felt conflicted. I thought I should be doing certain things, but I felt drawn to other things. This was a time of particular confusion brought on by confronting death, an experience that rocks you to your very core, but we all experience inner conflicts in different ways. I often go to a restaurant and when I look at the menu I really want a burger and fries, and yet, usually I end up having a salad with grilled salmon. But there is an inner struggle that takes place between when I first glance over the menu and when I give the waiter my order. For example, maybe you have a savings plan, but toward the end of the month you see something in a store that you really want to buy. To buy or not to buy? This creates another situation of inner conflict.

Usually in these moments, we know what we should do. We know which of the options will lead to long-term sustainable happiness, but we are attracted to the momentary pleasures. But some things can begin as pleasure and transform into unhappiness. Alcohol use can begin as pleasure and become misery. Apparent goods, things that appear to be good and pleasurable but in fact bring misery and unhappiness, often deceive us. They may seem

good because they are attractive, seductive, pleasurable, or entic-
ing, but when you overindulge in them, you lack a certain peace
within yourself—it's as though you are traveling without a ticket
and anxious because you might be discovered. More often than not
apparent goods deceive us simply because we act impulsively and
don't take enough time to reflect upon what we are about to do.

The bottom line is that when we act against our beliefs, we
begin to create a division within ourselves. When we lie, for example, we create an artificial division between our beliefs and our actions, and this division creates an inner conflict and a feeling of
being divided.

The corresponding reality is that we live in a world where people
seem to be acting contrary to their beliefs with an ever-increasing
frequency, so many of us are living divided lives. A divided life always has its roots in the betrayal of self. We abandon our beliefs,
and we justify it to ourselves and abdicate responsibility with a
thousand excuses: "I was unfaithful to my wife because she wasn't
attentive enough to me." "I lied about my income because taxes are
too high. Besides, everyone lies about their income. The only people who don't are those who can't, and if they could, they would."
"All my friends were doing it, so I figured I might as well give it a
try." In these acts, large or small, what is really taking place is a
betrayal of self. When we abandon our beliefs, we abandon our
selves.

The divided life has its attraction, no question, otherwise we
would not be drawn to it in the first place, but it also comes at a
very real cost to ourselves and to the people around us. The cost to
ourselves manifests as everything from restlessness, dis-ease, a reduced ability to contribute positively to society, and an inability to
experience joy to the denial of selfhood, a general discontented-
ness, and the inability to engage in meaningful relationships.
These are serious costs.

Many people, when confronted about the dividedness of their lives, will use the great excuses that we discussed earlier: "This is my life and I can do whatever I want" and "Leave me alone—this is just who I am." But as we discovered in chapter three, there are no strictly personal acts. If we elect to live a divided life by betraying ourselves, it will inevitably affect the lives of the people around us, even the lives of people we may never meet.

One of the great, gentle, humble voices of our age, Parker Palmer, wrote, "Dividedness is a personal pathology, but it soon becomes a problem for other people." We are witnesses to this phenomenon in business, in the classroom, in hospitals, in domestic and international politics, in families, and in our most intimate relationships. Our world is filled with the inevitable consequences of divided lives: violence, political corruption, broken relationships, economic injustice, environmental ruin, and war. All of these are the external expressions of our internal dividedness. When we betray ourselves we create havoc and misery for ourselves and for others. Eight hundred years ago, the poet Rumi said it in this way: "If you are unfaithfully with us / you're causing terrible damage."

The cost of the divided life is devastating and enormous. And yet, even in the midst of all of this, two good things remain: our desire to be whole and the voice that can lead us to that wholeness.

For years people have been asking me how it is possible at such a young age to write about the things I write about. There are many answers to that question. I have spent countless hours in the classroom of silence since I was in my late teens, and I continue to learn more each year in the silence than I do from books. I have had the extraordinary privilege of traveling in more than fifty countries, and that exposure to humanity in so many very different cultures has been an unmatched education in the universal struggles and qualities of people. And while I value silence, I also have an insatiable appetite for reading and studying and learning new things in all areas, from philosophy and science to business and personal development. Over the years, I have also refined a unique ability to observe myself and others, and from these observations I am able to derive the common traits of our human nature. But the part of the answer I rarely share with people is that a great deal of what I write is born from my own inner struggles. The fact that I write about these things with sometimes uncanny clarity doesn't mean that I do not face inner struggles myself. It would be a mistake to think that I sit here in my study and write these words from an imaginary wellspring of ideas. If I write about anything with great clarity, it is probably because I have struggled with these things more than most.

My struggle is in my yearning to move beyond the divided life. I yearn to be whole. I have personally experienced the divided life. On more occasions than I can comfortably recall, I have betrayed myself. And still I emerge from all of this with an undiminished yearning to live a life of integrity. This yearning is not diminished. It grows stronger and stronger.

I have no illusions about some kind of robotic perfection toward which we should all advance. But I yearn for the wholeness that allows me to embrace who I am and at the same time strive to achieve all I am capable of achieving and become all I am capable of becoming. This wholeness is made up of contentment and longing—the contentment with who we are today and the longing to improve ourselves for tomorrow. The key to healthy relationships with ourselves and with others is in seeking the delicate balance that allows both to coexist.

The key to creating this balance is aligning our actions with our beliefs. The words fall so easily to the page as I write them, but this is the constant struggle in my life—and yours, I suspect. When

I live my life separated from my beliefs, I am unhappy, and so I remain convinced that enduring happiness cannot be found except by uniting our actions with our beliefs.

Are you living a life in tune with your beliefs, or are you leading a divided life?

THE VOICE OF THE AUTHENTIC SELF

It would seem, then, that the great challenge is to work out what we believe. This is surprisingly easy. When it comes to everyday dilemmas, we all have a guide that is never wrong and often ignored. The voice of the authentic self calls to us ceaselessly from within. Traditionally it has been called the voice of conscience, but regardless of what name we give it, we all have this quiet, gentle voice within us, and it is our truest guide.

We are constantly overwhelmed by voices—the voices of parents, of friends, teachers, mentors, coaches, siblings, employers, experts, celebrities, politicians, preachers, advisors, consultants. All these voices make it very easy to drown out the quiet voice within. But this voice within is the voice of your authentic self. This is the-best-version-of-yourself talking to you. This is the voice of integrity, the voice of character, the voice of virtue. This is quite possibly the only voice in your life that has no agenda other than seeing you become perfectly yourself.

Identifying a set of core beliefs and developing a personal mission statement are powerful and useful exercises, but it is the voice within more than anything or anyone else that will help you to discover what you believe. Not all at once, though we wish it could be so, but step by step along the way. If you learn to listen to the gentle voice within you, it will grow stronger and stronger, and if you live by what you hear, that voice will grow clearer and clearer with every passing day.

Just because you are lost, doesn't mean your compass is broken. The voice of the authentic self will help you to heal the wounds created by living a divided life, by counseling you moment by moment, one situation at a time, to act in accord with what is good, true, noble, and beautiful. And by bringing your actions back into agreement with your beliefs, you will begin to create a new harmony in your life.

The second lesson for enduring happiness was "Just do the next right thing." How do we know what the next right thing to do is? By listening to the voice of our authentic self, the gentle but persistent voice within. The third lesson for enduring happiness was "Put character first." How do we put character first? By aligning our actions with the convictions of our hearts. It is this union between belief and action that brings about a life of integrity.

We often make light of the cliché "listen to your heart" as being overly sentimental or cheesy. This is in part due to the fact that the theme has been played upon so long and so often. But in most clichés there is a nugget of unchanging and universal truth. We would do well to overcome our bias toward this cliché and take the counsel of our hearts more seriously.

Every year thousands of people seek my counsel on issues ranging from relationships to business to politics, and from raising children to chasing down personal dreams. More than ninety percent of them already know what it is they should do in their particular circumstances. Most of the time we seek counsel because we lack the courage to do what we know we ought to do, because we hope someone might be able to talk us out of some situation that we know we must inevitably face if we are to be at peace with ourselves, or because we simply desire the solidarity of knowing that someone else knows the situation we are in the middle of. None of this is to say that we should not seek counsel, nor do I mind being the counsel whom so many people seek. But I don't know anybody who ever relied on their inner voice too much. Most of us err in the other direction—seeking the counsel of the authentic self too seldom.

The voices of the world can be very seductive, but they are no substitute for the gentle voice within. It was Plato's counsel that "the unexamined life is not worth living." Let us resolve to take some time each day to withdraw from the crazy, noisy, busy world into the sanctuary of the classroom of silence to work out who we are, what we believe, and what we are here for. Let us resolve at this very moment to take more time to listen to the gentle voice within and reflect on what is happening within us. If we feed and nurture our inner life, our outer life will blossom.

If you do nothing else in this lifetime, learn to listen to the gentle voice within you. It will lead you and if you follow you will live a life uncommon.

UNITY OF LIFE

This is what we long for: unity of life. What is unity of life? It is the sense that our life is one—not many parts or many compartments, but one living, breathing, ordered life. Unity of life gives birth to inner peace. It is the opposite of the conflicted and divided feeling that we were discussing earlier in this chapter. Unity of life is the result of aligning our actions with our beliefs, and it leads to a life of integrity, a life that is whole, a life that is undivided.

Between 1953 and 1981, Peace Pilgrim walked more than twenty-five thousand miles across the United States, spreading her simple message of peace. She talked with people on dusty roads and city streets, to college, church, and civic groups, on TV and radio, discussing peace within and peace in the world. In her writings about inner peace, she spoke of four preparations. The second is of particular interest to us at this time:

The second preparation has to do with bringing our lives into harmony with the laws that govern this universe. If we are out of harmony through ignorance, we suffer somewhat; but if we know better and are still out of harmony, then we suffer a great deal. I recognized that these laws are well-known and well-believed, and therefore they just needed to be well-lived.

So I got busy on a very interesting project. This was to live all the good things I believed in. I did not confuse myself by trying to take them all at once, but rather, if I was doing something that I knew I should not be doing, I stopped doing it, and I always made a quick relinquishment. You see, that's the easy way. Tapering off is long and hard. And if I was not doing something that I knew I should be doing, I got busy on that. Now if I believe something, I live it. Otherwise it would be perfectly meaningless. No life can be in harmony unless belief and practice are in harmony.

If we ever wish to have harmony in our lives, inner peace, and unity of life, we must begin the work of uniting our actions with our beliefs. In our quest for enduring happiness, it is important that we constantly remind ourselves that happiness is not achieved by the pursuit of happiness but rather is the result of right living. Right living, a life of integrity, is achieved by living through our daily actions all the good things we believe.

The problem we face is that we live in a society where duplicity is encouraged. Doctors are encouraged to leave their personal beliefs at the operating room door, teachers are told to leave their beliefs at the classroom door, and for the sake of party unity politicians are told to betray their own beliefs on certain issues, and the examples are endless. All of this duplicity is called for in the name of unity, but in truth it is dividing us and destroying us.

You cannot leave your ethics and beliefs at the door of your workplace and still hope to live a life of harmony and unity. You cannot set certain values and beliefs aside when you are socializing with certain friends and hope to maintain your inner peace. Character and beliefs are not a light switch to be turned on and off or a coat and hat to be left in the waiting room. They are part of the very fabric of our being. And when we treat them as optional accessories or disposable, we create deep divisions within ourselves.

Personal integrity—living by our beliefs, proactively willing the good of others, doing what we say we will do—is at the very core of unity of life. How then does one begin to create this unity of life?

Unity of life is established one decision at a time. In each moment, we must take the time to listen to that quiet and gentle voice within us and act in accord with what we hear. Most of the time we know what the right thing for us to do is. I am always amazed how if a child of four to six years old comes to you and says, "Can I do . . . ?" and you ask, "Will it help you to become the-best-version-of-yourself?" She knows instantly. She is not unfamiliar with all she is capable of being. She is not unfamiliar with what is good for her and what is not. The voice of the authentic self is probably stronger in young children than in the rest of us, who have been ignoring it for years and years.

Are you the same person at work as you are at home? Are you a different person with your friends than you are with your pastor? If the people in your life got together and talked about you, would they think they were talking about different people? The temptation is to compartmentalize our lives—to place work over here and family life over there, our beliefs and spirituality in another corner, and our social life over to one side. This compartmentalization creates the dividedness within us that is the enemy of inner peace.

Unity of life creates the sense that there is continuity among the different aspects of our lives and personalities. As we strive to bring our lives back into harmony with all that we believe to be good and true, there is no discounting the role of accountability and the power of friendship. We have a great ability to deceive ourselves. We make justifications and rationalizations in a vain attempt to convince ourselves that our duplicity is advantageous, manageable, harmless, or just plain necessary. There are aspects of the journey that must be faced alone, time in the classroom of silence to work out who we are and what we are here for and solitary moments of decision. But in general the burden of the journey is too great to bear all on our own. We need the help of others. People thrive in healthy communities. Whether a community is as small as a family or as large as a nation, its health rests in its willingness to encourage and support each member to thrive by becoming perfectly him- or herself.

Sooner or later, we rise or fall to the level of our friendships. There is no substitute in a person's life for friends of character and integrity.

It is extraordinary that in this day and age, in a time when so many technological advances have been made, there are still fifty thousand people dying each day in Africa from preventable disease and extreme poverty. Fifty thousand people. Real people, really dying, every day. Run your finger around the globe, and you can find countless examples of such poverty and injustice. But in developed nations, the great poverty is a poverty of genuine friendship. We need friends who help to make us whole, not friends who add to our dividedness. In fact, doesn't the word *friend* suggest something positive and good? I think the word in many cases is used too loosely. A true friend is one who helps you to become a-better-version-of-yourself, one who encourages you and challenges you, one who listens to you but also holds you accountable.

Among the people with whom I speak at seminars and correspond, the great frustration is that once they decide to walk a new path and make the journey back to their authentic self, they find it very lonely. Many people fall from this path simply because they cannot find anyone to make the journey with. And only the rare soul can make this journey alone. We need support and encouragement, but we also need accountability if we are going to restore and maintain unity in our lives. Seek out a few close friends to accompany you along the way. Be honest with each other and cherish each other, because friendships that help us become more perfectly ourselves are perhaps the rarest beauty in our modern culture.

And so we find ourselves at a crossroads. Will we continue to live our divided lives or will we seek wholeness of integrity by creating unity among the different aspects of our lives?

Divided no more. Isn't that how we all long to feel? Don't you long to feel whole? Consciousness and choice are what we must grapple with if we are to find wholeness. They are the source of the division and the unity, the source of our brokenness and our healing. The mere fact that we are aware of our dividedness, that we can acknowledge our need for unity in and of itself, is amazing and powerful. That is consciousness. And now we can respond to what we have become aware of and observed in ourselves and our lives. That response is choice. We can choose a new way and move toward the undivided life or we can ignore what we have discovered and bury ourselves in our dividedness.

The inner conflict and dividedness that plague so many lives is the result of living our lives contrary to the good things we believe. Are you living a double life? A triple life? A quadruple life? Are you living one life at school, another at work, one at home, one at church, and another with your friends? Are you one person when you are with some people and another person when you are with others? How many lives are you living?

THE PROBLEM IS NOT THAT WE DON'T BELIEVE

Beliefs play a powerful role in our lives. They cannot be confined to any one aspect of our experience in this world, and once we have given ourselves to certain beliefs, it is impossible to ignore them without doing great damage to ourselves and the people around us. That is why it is so important for us to take on beliefs with great caution. Gautama Buddha wrote, "Believe nothing merely because you have been told it. But believe what, after due examination and analysis, you find to be conducive to the welfare of all beings."

The problem is not that we do not believe but rather that we do not live what we believe. Most people have a set of values and beliefs that would greatly benefit the common good if they actually lived what they believed. But we often become so busy that we allow fatigue and stress to settle into our lives. This inevitably leads to a betrayal of self in ways small or large. Maintaining character requires constant vigilance and great strength and is all but impossible if we allow fatigue and stress to settle into our lives permanently.

What we believe affects everything: how we live, how we work, how we feel about ourselves, and how we feel about others. And in some ways it is impossible to hide our beliefs. Your life is a readout of what you believe. Sooner or later, every internal reality seeks an external expression. Spending time with your family is an external expression of the internal belief that spending time with your family is important. Being aggressive and rude to people is an external expression of an internal belief that other people have less value or dignity than you, or a fear that they have more value than you.

But all in all, experience leads me to believe that people are intrinsically good, that they would rather live with each other's happiness than misery, and that when their survival is not threatened people will go out of their way to help others. If we lived the good things we believe, the world would be remarkably different, an amazing place for our children and grandchildren to live and grow strong. The people on the other side of every conflict are more like you and me than they are different. Their hearts are filled with hopes and dreams just like yours and mine, they have been broken and bruised by life just as you and I have, and they seek a richer, brighter tomorrow just as we do.

———————

The fifth lesson for enduring happiness is this:

LIVE WHAT YOU BELIEVE.

We are constantly having to make decisions, hundreds of them every day. It is impossible to gather and analyze all the information and sift through the opinions of all the experts for each and every decision. The more complex our lives become, the more we need to accede to the gentle voice within.

In a world that is constantly and rapidly changing, the question we each have to ask ourselves is: What do I have in my life that is unchanging? Because it is what is unchanging that allows us to make sense of change. It is what is unchanging that allows us to thrive in the midst of change. For a moment, reflect on the life of the United States of America as a nation. What has allowed this nation to thrive in the midst of periods of rapid change? The Constitution. Yes, there have been amendments along the way, but the core of the Constitution remains unchanged. It is what is unchanging that allows us to make sense of the change. When America is faced with an opportunity or a crisis, it looks to the Constitution for guidance. In situations of change and uncertainty, the only reliable sources of navigation are those that are constant and unchanging. The Constitution is the North Star in America's sky.

Our core beliefs play a very similar role in our own lives. They guide us in times of uncertainty and confusion. They allow us to thrive in the midst of constantly changing environments at home, at work, at school, in relationships, and in society. That is why it is so important that we take time to step into the classroom of silence on a regular basis and reflect on what matters most and what we believe. Only then will we be able to keep the counsel of the voice of the authentic self that whispers to us night and day from within . . . and only then will we begin to establish the unity of life that gives birth to integrity, inner peace, and enduring happiness.

It is one thing not to believe something; it is something completely different and debilitating to believe and not live in that belief. Old-fashioned as it may seem to people, there is a lot of restlessness and dis-ease in our lives that could be quickly cured by a clear conscience. Let us start to live all the good things we believe.

LIVE WHAT YOU BELIEVE

I will apply the fifth lesson of enduring happiness
to my life by taking the following steps:

1. I will begin to live all the good things I believe, being mindful that when I act contrary to my beliefs, I invite unhappiness into my life and the lives of others. If there is something that I know I should not be doing, I will stop doing it immediately. I will begin to regularly access what I believe and allow my beliefs to direct my words, thoughts, and actions.

2. I will seek the healthy balance that allows me to be content with who I am today while at the same time longing to improve tomorrow. I will do this by rejecting the generic perfection that is so often celebrated in our culture and strive in each moment to create wholeness by being perfectly myself.

3. I will recognize friendship as a remarkable gift and responsibility by establishing clearly in my mind that the primary purpose of every friendship is to help each other become better-versions-of-ourselves. I will seek out and nurture friendships that elevate me, encourage me, challenge me, and bring me to life. And I will be mindful of relationships that drain my energy and encourage me to betray myself, distancing myself from these relationships when necessary. I will endeavor to encourage others to live all the good things they believe and I will surround myself with people who encourage me to celebrate my authentic self.

4. When I feel conflicted or divided, I will pause to determine how my words, thoughts, or actions have strayed from my beliefs. I will celebrate these feelings of dividedness and inner conflict because they remind me of my desire to be whole. I will connect with my desire for wholeness and seek to establish greater integrity in all areas of my life.

Six

Beyond Instant Gratification

Our culture often prescribes instant gratification as a cure for our deep desire for happiness. As a result we often fall into the trap of believing that we would be happy if we could just do what we feel like doing right at any given moment. Our insatiable appetite for instant gratification tends to lead us farther and farther away from character, virtue, integrity, wholeness, and our authentic self. Coupled with our untamed affinity with instant gratification is our mistaken notion that freedom is the right or ability to do whatever we want. I meet people all the time who tell me they want to start their own business. When I ask them why, I expect to hear that they want to do something they are more passionate about or because they want to be involved in more meaningful work. But the most common response I get is that then they won't have a boss telling them what to do. High school students are always complaining about the limitations placed on them by parents and teachers.

Do we really believe that a life without structure or discipline will yield the happiness we desire? Besides, how successful do you suppose your business would be if you just did whatever you wanted whenever you wanted to? What sort of financial shape would you be in if you bought whatever you wanted, whenever you wanted it? How good would your health be if you ate as much as you wanted, of whatever you wanted, whenever you wanted it? How healthy would your relationships be if you did what you felt like doing only when you felt like doing it?

A life without self-discipline doesn't lead to happiness—it leads to ruin. Every area of our life—physical, emotional, intellectual, spiritual, professional, and financial—benefits from self-discipline. Does that mean we should never engage in instant gratification? No. But it does mean that we cannot allow instant gratification to guide and direct every decision. We need to move beyond the notion that discipline is someone else telling us what to do and celebrate the self-discipline that liberates us. How much discipline is enough? The answer depends on how happy you want to be, and for how long you want that happiness to last.

THE HAPPINESS MYTH

I have a friend who is in the infomercial business, and I am always amused to hear about which infomercials are successful. They seem to focus on four main areas: food and diet, exercise, money, and relationships. All of them promise different types of "happiness," and it is staggering how many people are buying. Let's take a look at each of the four areas and the promises that are made, one at a time.

Last year, Americans spent three hundred billion dollars on diet products. That's outrageous when you consider this figure is larger than the gross domestic product of many nations. It's even more outrageous when you consider that the only diet most people need is a little bit of discipline. But that's the point. Let's be clear about what we are buying. We don't want discipline, we want someone to get on the television and tell us that we can be happy without discipline. Turn the television on any hour of the day or night and just start flipping through the channels. You'll encounter the guy who tells you that if you take this tablet he is selling three times a day, every day, you can eat as much as you want of whatever you want as often as you want, and you will still look like a supermodel.

If it's not the guy with his tablets, it's the woman with her little mats, and what does she say? "Just lie down!" I mean, how hard could it be? She tells you to just lie down on her mat for twenty minutes twice a week. We will call it Pilates, and she promises that if you do, you can eat whatever you want and still look like a supermodel.

Then of course we have the guy on his flying exercise machine. He has the body of a Greek god and assures you that you can too if you will ride his machine for twenty minutes three times a week. The phones are ringing off the hook, and it's the most successful infomercial in history. But do you really believe that he got the body he has by riding that machine for twenty minutes three times a week?

Flip through a couple more channels, and now you'll see the real estate charlatan promising that you can buy all the property you want with no money down and that within sixty days you can have positive cash flow of twenty thousand dollars a month. Have you ever purchased property? How long does it take to find one, negotiate a price, arrange financing, have the property inspected, schedule the closing, and so on? Hold on a minute! There is some fine print along the bottom of the screen. What does it say? In print that is so small you wonder if it isn't just a line across the bottom of the screen, print that I might mention is white on white so as not to enhance viewers' chance of reading it, it says that results will vary from person to person.

But perhaps what is really bothering you at the moment is your relationship, so you begin to flip channels again. In quick succession you encounter women in bikinis telling you to pick up the phone and dial a 900 number if you are lonely, then an advertisement for an online dating service that promises to connect you with someone perfectly suited to you, and then a psychologist who promises that his program will empower you to find a person who gives you everything you want, whenever you want it, and expects nothing in return. Isn't it unreasonable and irrational to even desire a relationship that matches this description?

Is it that we are gullible? I don't think so. I think it is desperation. We are desperate to keep the dominant myth of our culture alive. What do all of these infomercials have in common? What is the common lie? They all make it sound fun and easy, and none of them speak of discipline and hard work. The common lie in all of these programs is that you can be happy without discipline. It is the myth that is driving our culture, and we will pay any amount of money to keep it alive, because the alternative seems too daunting to us.

The common denominator of all successful diets is discipline. You know what foods are good for you and which are not. Choose those that are good for you and eat in moderation. You'll be healthier and happier. The common denominator of every successful financial plan is discipline. Create a budget, control spending, save, and invest. The common denominator of all successful relationships is discipline. It takes real discipline to be aware and responsive to the physical, emotional, intellectual, and spiritual needs of another person. The common denominator of successful exercise routines is discipline. The common denominator of successful careers is discipline. The common denominator of successful organizations is discipline.

And a large factor in that discipline is consistency. Health, wealth, careers, organizations, relationships, all require consistency if they are going to thrive for any length of time.

Our lives have become overrun by experts and programs. We are smart people. We don't need half the experts and programs that we have in our lives, but we do need discipline. And all the programs and experts are no substitute for it.

You cannot be happy without discipline. In fact, if you want to measure the level of happiness in your life, measure your level of discipline. You will never have more happiness than you have discipline. The two are directly linked to each other. If you want to increase the level of fulfillment and happiness in a certain area of your life, increase your level of discipline in that area of your life. On the other hand, if you find that you are altogether too happy too much of the time, you may want to think about decreasing the level of discipline in your life. Discipline and happiness are directly linked.

How Long Is Your Fuse?

Self-control is the ingredient that the products, programs, and experts cannot sell us. Self-control is a gift that we give to ourselves and is the very essence of discipline. We are not born with it; it is acquired. We acquire it by practicing it. Let us focus our discussion of self-control on three areas: temper, appetites, and impulses.

From time to time you will hear someone say, "Oh don't mind her—she just has a short fuse!" This comment usually comes as an excuse for some type of tantrum or outburst, and is offered as if having a bad temper was some type of genetically inalterable state.

Why is it that some people fly off the handle at the smallest things and other people seem to possess the patience of Job? Are we born with our fuse length preset? Honestly, I don't know. But what I do know is that we can lengthen or shorten our fuse length. We can choose if we are going to be the person throwing the temper tantrums or the person patiently enduring the inevitable disappointments of life. People don't have bad tempers; they have badly trained tempers.

There is a moment of decision between when something upsets us and our reaction to it. In that moment we actually decide how we will react, whether or not we are aware that we are making the decision. With practice, we can increase our awareness of that moment and start to draw it out by conscious effort. By doing so, we allow ourselves to make an intelligent decision about the appropriate response. We can use that moment to breathe deeply or leave the room to compose ourselves.

I have seven brothers, and as you can imagine, as children we could be quite a handful from time to time. When we went altogether too far, my mother would send us all to the laundry room. That meant we were going to get a spanking, usually with a wooden spoon. We couldn't all fit into the laundry room, so some of us would sit around outside. Nobody wanted to be first, because everybody knew she would be tired by the time she got to the end, but sometimes she started with those inside the laundry room and sometimes with those outside.

Having sent us to the laundry room, my mother would then go and make herself a cup of coffee and sit at the kitchen table and drink it slowly before coming to spank us. I asked her several years later why she used to do this, and she told me that she used to get so angry at times and that she never wanted to beat us out of anger, but she needed to spank us out of love.

Self-control is always accompanied by self-awareness. As we become more and more aware of ourselves and of the way we react to certain types of people and situations, our ability to control our response increases. The moment between event and response is where we choose how we are going to react. People with short fuses are almost completely oblivious to the moment because their temper-filled reactions have shortened with practice.

A short temper is a habit that has been chosen and can be changed. Anger is a natural and normal part of our human makeup. I think people love the passage in the Bible where Jesus goes into the temple and turns over the money changers' tables. It reveals a very human side of Jesus that people can relate to. There are times when anger should be expressed and expressed powerfully. But they are rare. Like any passion, for anger to be useful it has to be harnessed, controlled, and directed at will.

Technology is helping us do things faster and faster, but our fuses seem to be getting shorter and shorter. Once upon a time, the dial-up Internet connection was miraculous. Today it is a dinosaur. The connections just keep getting faster and faster, but they never seem fast enough. Overnight delivery used to be a fast way to get things somewhere; now we need it delivered before 8 AM the next day. It seems nothing is fast enough anymore, or is it just that our fuses are not long enough?

Do you need to work on increasing the length of your fuse? Most of us do. We live in a culture of instant gratification. We are used to getting what we want when we want it, so when things don't go our way, the fuse begins to burn.

Interestingly, we can usually predict the people and situations that are going to cause us to lose our temper. We are aware of them even before they happen. We may not know when they are going to happen or even if they are going to happen, but we have some awareness of them. That awareness is a powerful gift. In the last chapter, I spoke about consciousness and choice. We are dealing with exactly the same thing here. These are two of the great powers of the human mind and spirit.

Awareness is a form of consciousness, and choice is our response to certain events. We have all met people who are completely unaware of the way their manner affects other people. We see this in alcoholics and other addicts all the time. The nature of their addiction turns them in on themselves, makes them completely self-involved, and erroneously places them at the center of the universe. They can't understand why the people around them can't just lighten up. They often throw temper tantrums. The more they drink, the less awareness they have of who they are, what they are doing, and how it is affecting the people around them. And the more their awareness decreases, the shorter their fuse gets. They often become loud, abusive, argumentative, and sometimes violent. This is one extreme example, but a more common example is people who just talk and talk and talk with no regard for whether the person they are speaking to is interested or listening. This is another form of diminished self-awareness.

How long is your fuse? From time to time, people will ask, "Do you have a temper?" The truth is that we all have a temper. The real questions are: Are you able to control your temper? Are you in control of your temper? Or is your temper in control of you?

Each person has a temperament. It could be argued that temperament is the result of a combination of nature and nurture, but it is agreed that a person's temperament can be altered by effort. An impatient man can become a patient man by practicing patience. A woman with a short fuse and a wild temper can become a woman with a long fuse and a capacity to silently endure unfavorable circumstances. A greedy and covetous man can become a generous man, and so on. Our temperaments are not set at birth; they are changeable by choice and consciousness.

Your temperament is your default position. It is your baseline. It is your emotional home base. Is it unpredictable and fiery? Is it calm and unhurried? Is it selfish and thoughtless? Is it generous and kind? Whatever it is, whatever your default position, it is what it is because you have practiced the qualities that make it so. The good news is that you can change it.

As a teenager, I had quite a temper. I was always in the face of the referee on the soccer field, wondering aloud if he got his badge from a corn flakes box. I remember one day when my father gave me a talking-to on the way home from a game, explaining that I wore his name and my seven brothers wore the same name, and that my actions were unbecoming of the name that I wore and reflected badly on us all. I was at times even worse on the golf course. I took myself altogether too seriously and would lose my temper at the drop of a hat, a habit that affects my golfing game more than any other factor. I would bang clubs on the ground, throw clubs, and yes, even break clubs on occasion. I look back now and wonder where that person went.

In my late teen years I was exposed to some extraordinary coaches and mentors who taught me the way of character and the power of virtue in our lives. One golf coach in particular told me that I would never become a good golfer if I didn't learn to control my temper, and that if I didn't show signs of improvement immediately, he would not work with me. He then gave me a number of exercises to help improve my patience and increase the length of my fuse—breathing exercises that seem fairly simple and rudimentary in hindsight, but nobody had ever shown me such a thing. But the one that had the biggest impact on me was the exercise that required me simply to sit still. Every day, I was to sit still on a chair for thirty minutes—completely still, no movement other than the rising and falling of my breath. If I got an itch on my leg I was to ignore it. "It won't kill you," he would say. The itch would get worse, and then after a while it would go away. The spirit was rising above the body. I was developing strength of mind and heart, increasing my self-control. My fuse was getting longer, and sure enough this made me a better golfer.

The question is not "What is your temperament?" but rather "What would you like your temperament to be?" In *The Rhythm of Life,* I wrote about learning to walk like a man who doesn't have a care in the world. I would like to be able to become more and more like that man, a man who walks calmly, thinks calmly, and acts calmly, even under pressure—especially under pressure.

THE MODERN TYRANT

Self-control is the foundation of discipline and a prerequisite for character, integrity, happiness, and, as we will discover later in this chapter, love and dynamic relationships. The first area of self-control deals with temper and temperament. These are concerned very much with a certain mastery of the mind. The second area of self-control concerns our appetites and the body.

The human person is a delicate composition of body and soul that is carefully linked by the will and the intellect. Most of the animal kingdom lives directed by instincts and conditioned responses. As human beings, we have consciousness and choice in a way that animals do not, and these are what set us apart. But we also have instincts, and for better or for worse, we are capable of conditioned responses, though because we possess the higher faculties of will and intellect, we can choose which responses we want to become conditioned to. Furthermore, we are aware of which responses are good for us and which are self-destructive. Nowhere is this more apparent than in our ability to control our physical appetites.

The body is amazing and wonderful, but left to its own instincts and devices, it will tend toward the self-destruction of a million excesses and unbridled lusts. That's why we have will and intellect, consciousness, and the ability to make choices, so that we can direct the body toward what is good for it. But that is not exactly how it works out in our practical, everyday lives, now is it? Why? Because the body has a voice. The body talks to us, screams at us, throws internal temper tantrums, and makes an unending list of requests and demands. We have the ability to ignore this voice, but too often we do just exactly what it tells us to do.

First thing when you wake up in the morning, the body says, *I'm still tired.* So you slap the snooze button and go back to sleep. Seven minutes later, the body says, *I'm still tired!* So you slap the snooze button again.

When you finally do haul yourself out of bed, the body says, *I'm hungry.* So you feed it. Then the body says, *I'm thirsty.* So you give it a drink. Now the body says, *I feel sort of icky!* So you throw it in the shower. The body says, *Too cold.* Then *Too hot.* Then *Let's stay in here for five more minutes.* When you get out of the shower, the body says, *I'm wet.* So you dry it. Then it says, *I'm cold and naked.* So you clothe it.

All too often, you do what the body tells you to do. The body says, *If we are going to get through this day, I am going to need a nice big cup of black poison.* So you go downstairs and get your coffee brewed hot and strong. The body takes a sip of that and says, *Mmmmmm . . . now we're ready for life.*

When you get to work, the body says, *I don't feel like working. Maybe we could just walk around and say hello to everybody.* So you walk around catching up on the latest office gossip and politics. You pass the break room. And what's in the break room? Yes, fifty-six varieties of doughnuts. You think to yourself, *I might have one of those doughnuts,* but the body says, *No you won't. We'll have four of those doughnuts.* So you grab a handful of doughnuts and take them back to your desk. The body says, *And while you're at it, get me some more black poison.*

You drink your coffee and eat your doughnuts, and before you know it, it's noon. The body cries out, *It's lunchtime!* You explain to the body that you are not hungry because you have been snacking all morning, but the body says, *It doesn't matter if you are hungry or not. It's lunchtime. Let's go to lunch now.*

You go to lunch by yourself or with some friends and you eat more food than you should have eaten even if you hadn't eaten in a month. When you get back to work the body says, *Food coma! Food coma!* You sit at your desk shuffling papers in a bit of a daze for a couple of minutes, and then the body says, *If we are going to do anything this afternoon, you'd better make it light and easy. Maybe we could just sit here at the desk and fiddle around on the Internet and pretend that we're working.*

Then all of a sudden the body has an idea: *Get me some snacks and some more black poison.*

You're in a food coma. What do you need snacks for? you bravely question your body.

The body replies, *Well, I can't fall asleep while I'm eating, can I?* You get some snacks and some more coffee, and this goes on throughout the afternoon. At about 3 PM, the body demands some more black poison, but of the cold variety now . . . whatever type of cola is available.

Before you know it, it's time to go home. The body demands, *Get me some snacks for the trip home.*

You argue, *We're going home for dinner.*

The body insists, *We could get stuck in a traffic jam. We could die of starvation in that traffic jam!* So you get some snacks for the ride home, and when you get home, it's not quite dinnertime. So you plant yourself in your recliner chair in front of your 127-inch idiot box again with a 300-ounce bag of potato chips, just to relax a little before dinner.

Then the body cries out, *It's dinnertime!* You're not hungry, but you got done arguing with the body about twelve hours earlier. So you take yourself off to dinner, and the body says, *We will have some of that and some of that and some of that and some more of that....* You eat more food than you should have eaten even if you weren't going to eat for another month. Then the body's food coma alert starts going off again, and the body says, *Let's go back to that recliner and relax.* Half an hour later, the body says, *I want some more black poison, but we'd better switch to decaf now 'cause it's getting late and I'm gonna wanna go to bed soon. And while you're at it, get me a nice big bowl of chocolate ice cream.*

You get the decaf and the ice cream, the body devours that, and then the body says, *Let's go to bed. I'm exhausted.* You haul the body off to bed. You wake up the next morning to do the same routine from dawn to dusk.

The body has a voice for a reason: to alert us to hunger, thirst, heat, cold, and danger. But when we overindulge the body, this voice becomes the voice of craving rather than the voice of need.

The body is like money, a horrible master but an excellent servant. Here in America, and certainly in my homeland of Australia, we generally consider ourselves to be free. We are absolutely kidding ourselves. We are not free. Most people can't go a day without a cup of coffee, yet we think we are free. We need to wake up. We don't need someone to come across the ocean and enslave us. We have enslaved ourselves. The great dictator of the twenty-first century will not be like Stalin or Hitler. The greatest threats are not external. The great dictator of the twenty-first century is the body. We do whatever it tells us to do, whenever it tells us to do it.

With every passing day, people's ability to control their appetites is rapidly diminishing, and this poses some serious threats to our health and happiness as individuals and as a society.

Again, the good news is that over time we can develop the ability to control our appetites. The appetites of the body are not preset and unchangeable. We may have preferences and established habits, but they can be changed. Learning to direct our appetites at will is a powerful aspect of personal discipline and self-control.

Self-mastery is the only alternative to the enslavement of self. We may not be imprisoned behind iron bars, but unless we can exercise and direct our appetites, the invisible bars that imprison us may be more harmful. In my visits to prisons around the world over the past decade, I have met men and women who have more self-possession and personal freedom than most people who are free to walk the streets at will.

THE POWER OF IMPULSE

From temperament and appetite, we now move to the third aspect of discipline, controlling our impulses. Impulses can relate to many aspects of our daily experience, but for the sake of variety let us focus our discussion here on personal finances.

I have a friend who for the sake of anonymity I will call Julia. She is twenty-eight, single, and talented. She has a good job and works hard, enjoys her work for the most part, makes a reasonable living. And though she doesn't earn a fortune, there are certainly plenty of families getting by on what she is making. Some of her friends make more money than she does and some make less.

Julia's problem is that she loves to shop, and every week she gets a new credit card offer in the mail. She loves to shop in stores, online, and from home catalogues. Some of her friends tell her she has a self-esteem problem that causes her to shop too much. Other friends tell her it's normal to want to shop like she does.

Once a year she sits down with her financial advisor, and every year, they have the same conversation, with this point: "You have to start saving, even if it is just a little bit each month. It really adds up over the years." So each year, they design a new budget for Julia, to take into account her annual pay raise, but for some reason Julia just cannot save any money. She doesn't have any debt—well, almost no debt. Just a little on this card and a little on that card. But she also doesn't have any savings or assets.

About the middle of each year, when she is completely failing at her budget and ashamed to go and see her financial advisor again, she comes to me. Julia tells me that she doesn't want to be rich, just comfortable. So I take her through some rudimentary scenarios. What would happen if you lost your job tomorrow and it took you three months to find another job? Would you be comfortable? She glares at me, but she also knows that what I am proposing is not too far-fetched, and we haven't even gotten into the whole list of more serious possibilities.

Then we have the discussion that shoes and clothes are not investments or assets. I explain again that a good asset or investment is something that creates cash flow. Shoes don't create any income. "But when I buy good shoes I always tell myself they are a good investment, because if I buy cheap shoes they fall apart and I need more," she explains. I wonder to myself how many pairs of shoes she would have if she bought "cheap" shoes, but by now she is not in a joking mood. I explain that they may be a good purchase, but that there is a difference between a good purchase and an investment. I then go on to explain that good purchases should be made within the confines of a budget, and that at a certain point saving is better than any purchase no matter how good we may perceive it to be.

At some point in our conversation, Julia usually begins to complain about the parts of her job she doesn't like or talk about how she doesn't want to do what she is doing forever or explain how her boss really gets on her nerves and how she would like to start her own business one day. All of this is usually a subconscious attempt to move away from the not-so-happy present reality and dream about a richer, more abundant future. But she walks her way straight back into the conversation about personal finances with the question "Do you think I would be able to borrow any money to start a business?"

"You already own your own business," I say to her.

"What do you mean?" she inquires.

I explain that she owns one hundred percent of the stock in a corporation called Julia Miles, Inc. Last year Julia Miles, Inc., spent more money than it earned. The year before that was the same, as was the year before that one. Every year her business is losing money, spending more money than it earns. It may just be a couple of hundred dollars here and there on outstanding credit cards, but she is operating at a loss every year. Julia Miles has not had a single profitable year since she graduated from college. Financially, she has nothing to show for the six years she has worked.

"I know I have to start saving!" she says, exasperated.

"Why can't you save?" I ask.

"I just see things I like and I have to have them."

Julia doesn't control her impulse to buy. We all have impulses, and for some the impulse to spend money is as powerful as a craving for a drug. Other people have powerful impulses to gamble and drink alcohol, to have sex and view pornography, to seek danger and adventure, and all can be massively self-destructive. But impulses, like tempers and appetites, can be controlled and directed for our own good and the good of others.

The real danger is that impulses and appetites can join together and quickly transform into compulsions and addictions. With our tempers, appetites, and impulses running free, we now live in a global community of addicts. Most of us tell ourselves that we don't have any of the big, serious addictions. For us it might be "just" cigarettes, chocolate, diet soda, or coffee. From time to time we wonder whether we are addicted to these things, but we usually are not short of excuses—and if we are, there is always a "friend" there to slap us on the back and tells us that we think too much.

The great Spanish mystic and monk, John of the Cross, wrote, "A bird, whether it is tied down by a thread or a chain, still cannot fly." What's tying you down? What is it in your life that is stopping you from flying?

A Path to Self-Mastery

There are few things of which I am absolutely certain, and over the years the list has become shorter and shorter. But one of the things that I am totally convinced of is that our level of discipline and self-control significantly affects the level of happiness we experience in this life. Mastery of self and happiness are intimately connected.

Many people have written about techniques for gaining this self-mastery, and throughout this chapter I have mentioned a few in passing. Authors and speakers tend to focus on techniques that are particularly related to their areas of professional focus. But is there a way to foster self-control that will affect all areas of our lives in a powerful and positive way?

I want to focus on an ancient technique that fosters this universal self-mastery and is largely ignored in the modern schema. It has been overlooked and unpopular, first because this technique is easily taught and cannot be sold as part of a package, and second because we often shy away from that which we need most, preferring programs that seem easier or more enjoyable. But this ancient technique drives right to the heart of our struggle to regain mastery of ourselves.

Much of our struggle with discipline and self-control is rooted in our appetites and impulses, and in many ways our undisciplined temperaments are an outgrowth of our inability to master our appetites and impulses. All of this stems from our obsession with the body, our placement of pleasure at the center of our value system, and a tendency to overlook the importance of character in our quest for happiness. As a result, we tend to overidentify with physical experience.

One of the great practices fostered in many spiritual traditions for thousands of years is fasting.

I am not suggesting we fast completely. In fact, I am not even suggesting the strict fast of bread and water of many traditions. What I am advocating is denying ourselves in small ways so that we can regain the self-mastery that makes us free and take control once more of our temperament, appetites, and impulses.

For a Buddhist monk, fasting is one part of the search for enlightenment. For thousands of years, it has been the practice of Jewish people to fast for atonement from their sins against God and neighbor. It has also long been a practice of Christians to fast in atonement for sins. Christians also believe that through fasting they begin to reverse the way their self-destructive behaviors of the past weakened their ability to choose what is good, true, and right. There are hundreds of other examples of how fasting has been used throughout history. In modern times, fasting has often been used as a spiritual-political tool, never more powerfully than when Gandhi fasted to bring warring factions together for his dream of a united and self-ruling India. And with a growing awareness of health and well-being, a number of detox programs include fasting as part of their regimen.

Fasting has been employed to liberate men and women from sin and oppression and from appetites, impulses, and wayward temperaments. In our discussion here we are particularly concerned with how this powerful and ancient spiritual practice might serve us in our quest to increase self-control and attain liberation from the habits of mind and body that prevent us from becoming perfectly ourselves.

Let us make no mistake that humankind's most noble state is freedom—not freedom from opposing political or religious thoughts and ideas but freedom to do what is good and right in the many and various situations that we face in the course of daily life. Our hearts never stop longing for this freedom. A woman who is dying of lung cancer and still cannot resist a cigarette is not free. A man who has diabetes and cannot stop eating candy is not free. A person who has been in and out of treatment for alcohol abuse but cannot stop drinking is not free. These are extreme cases to make the point, but most of us face more subtle expressions of this type of slavery. Perhaps you are trying to lose weight but cannot stop snacking between meals even when you are not hungry. Maybe you don't really need anything, but you cannot stop shopping.

Remember, whether a bird is tied down by a thread or by a chain, it still cannot fly. What is master of your life? What do you need to be liberated from?

So what do I mean by fasting, and how can it help?

I am not suggesting a bread and water fast for forty days as many mystics practiced annually in ancient times. But allow me to give a couple of simple examples of modern applications of the discipline of fasting.

Sometime next Saturday afternoon, you are wandering around at home and your body says, *I'm thirsty.* You head toward the refrigerator. On the way, your body starts to bark its demands. *How about a soda? I want a soda! Get me a soda!* You get to the fridge and open the door and the requests, suggestions, and demands of your body intensify. *I want a soda! Is there any soda in there? Look harder! There must be some soda in there! Look at the back. There's a soda. Get that soda. Hurry up. I'm thirsty. I want a soda. Get that soda. Soda! Soda! Soda! Soda! Soda!* This is how the body talks to us. It insists; it demands.

All you need to do is say to your body, *No soda today! You can have some cranberry juice or a glass of water, but no soda.* In that one simple action of the mind and spirit, you assert dominance over your body. By having cranberry juice or water when your body really craves soda, you set yourself free in a small way from the slavery of your body. It's not going to kill you, and nobody else knows that it has happened, but you have made a choice for a-better-version-of-yourself, and you will feel the liberation.

You go shopping next week and see something that you really like. You pick it up and look at it. You try it on or imagine where it would go in your home. Your impulses are excited, and they begin to chant, *Buy it! Buy it! Buy it!* You begin to walk toward the register, but then you stop for a moment. This is the moment between event and response. In the past, you saw it and you bought it, but now you ask yourself, *Do I really need this?* You know you don't, and that moment of awareness and reflection makes that abundantly clear. You put it back on the shelf and walk away. And as you walk away, you feel as free as a bird. It is so liberating that you feel it physically.

Fasting doesn't have to involve food. You can fast from shopping, you can fast from criticizing yourself and others, you can fast from complaining, you can fast from procrastination. You can fast from anything that causes you to become a slave of your temper, appetites, or impulses. But fasting in relation to food is particularly powerful in an age when we focus so much on eating and drinking.

Every time I sit down to eat a meal, I try to deny myself something. Perhaps I am at a restaurant, and as I read the menu I really begin to crave the filet mignon, so I have the chicken instead. It's not going to kill me. It's only food, fuel for the body, but we forget that sometimes and make altogether too much of a big deal out of it. Or perhaps I really feel like cranberry juice, but I have water with my meal instead. It is these small, simple, unseen acts that remind the body that it is my servant and not my master. I don't do these things to be mean to myself or to punish myself. I do them because I want to be free. I want to have control over myself. I want to be able to control my temper, my appetites, and my impulses. All of these tiny acts of self-denial expand that moment between event and response. This is another way for me to make my fuse longer.

It is in this way and many others that the ancient and spiritual practice of fasting has enormous relevance in our modern lives. The benefits range from improving our temperaments to creating dynamic and lasting relationships. The latter topic always seems to set off a natural curiosity in my audiences. How would fasting help create lasting and dynamic relationships?

Two people with long fuses are always going to have a better relationship than two people with short fuses. Two people with controlled and directed temperaments are always going to have a better relationship than two people with unbridled temperaments. Two people who have control over their appetites are always going to have a better relationship than two people who cannot control their appetites. And two people who are able to master their impulses are always going to have a better relationship than two people who are slaves to their impulses.

But the most compelling point for a life of discipline, character, virtue, integrity, and self-control is this: To the extent that you have these things you will be able to love and be loved, for to love is as if you could take your very self in your hands and give it to another person. But to give yourself in this way, you must first possess yourself.

Most people in relationships are making promises they cannot keep. They are promising to give themselves in ways they are simply not able to, because they do not possess themselves. They have no self-mastery and therefore they are not free. To love, we must be free. Only to the extent that we are able to wrench ourselves away from the slavery of temper, appetites, and impulses will we be able to love and be loved. This is why there is such a poverty of love and dynamic relationships in our culture, because for those addicted to instant gratification, a lasting relationship is an impossible dream.

I like nice things and wonderful food and spontaneous living as much as the next person. I am not proposing that we give up all the wonderful pleasures of this world, just that we temper our approach to them so that we can more fully savor them as we taste and experience them. It is time we sought freedom from the tyrants within that tie us up and tie us down, that stop us from flying and becoming perfectly ourselves.

The sixth lesson for enduring happiness is this:

BE DISCIPLINED.

Discipline makes us free. It doesn't stifle us. It liberates us. Discipline is a contraction that produces an expansion.

BE DISCIPLINED

I will apply the sixth lesson of enduring happiness
to my life by taking the following steps:

1. I will celebrate my ability to control my temper by consciously expanding the moment that exists between an event and my reaction to it. When things do not go as I would like them to, I will pause before reacting, breathe deeply, remind myself that in the grand scheme of human history this is just one moment, and walk away from the situation to collect myself if necessary. If a situation genuinely requires that I unleash my temper, it will be a conscious choice and it will be done in a controlled way. I will become master of my temper.

2. I will begin to control and direct my appetites. I will not allow myself to be reduced to a mere animal, being ruled by instincts and conditioned responses. I will celebrate my ability to choose which stimuli I respond to and which I ignore. I will direct my appetites toward those things that are good for me and genuinely help me to become my best self. I will avoid putting anything that is poisonous or toxic into my body. From this day on, I will respect my body as a great temple. I will become master of my appetites.

3. I will control my impulses. Recognizing that my impulses do not always lead me to become a-better-version-of-myself, I will develop a healthy distrust of my impulses and begin to subject them to reason. Whether the impulse is to shop, eat, procrastinate, or agree to attend an event, I will pause before acting on that impulse. I will become master of my impulses.

4. I recognize that it is impossible for me to be perfectly myself unless I am free. I will engage the ancient and powerful practice of fasting, not to punish myself but to liberate myself. I will begin to deny myself in small ways throughout the day, fasting from certain types of foods, certain activities, and certain behaviors. In this way, and over time, I will establish a complete and absolute self-mastery. On some days I may fast from chocolate, soda, coffee, or meat. On other days I will fast from gossip, criticism, or laziness. I will engage the power of fasting and self-denial to free myself from the slavery of my temper, appetites, and impulses. In this way I will become free to be most authentically myself.

5. From time to time I will allow myself to indulge in the things that my appetites and impulses yearn for, but only in ways that do not compromise what I believe and do not harm myself or others. On these occasions I will exercise my ability to direct my appetites and impulses, allowing them what they yearn for rather than denying them. In each case I will do so in such a way that does not compromise my self-mastery. Over time I will learn to see both indulgence and self-denial as acts that foster the discipline that gives birth to enduring happiness.

Seven

Unburden Yourself

Sometimes I like to go back and reread books from my child-hood. I often have very clear memories of how these books touched me when I first read them, and it never ceases to amaze me how far removed they are from the central themes of these books. A couple of weeks ago I picked up E. B. White's *Charlotte's Web*. The message that struck me was an entirely self-evident truth that we tend to overlook in our daily living, and it was contained in one simple line, "There's no limit to how complicated things can get on account of one thing always leading to another."

Clutter, congestion, and confusion have become an accepted part of most people's everyday experience of life, but it doesn't need to be that way. We have chosen and created the clutter and congestion. As hard as it may be to get our minds around at first, by creating the clutter and confusion we have created the confusion in our hearts, minds, and lives. It is a difficult truth, but a liberating one. All truth is, I suppose. But once we can bring ourselves to realize that we have chosen and created the clutter, congestion, and confusion of our lives, we are free to choose to be rid of it. Admitting that we had a role in the creation of a situation frees us from victimhood and empowers us to play a role in its re-creation.

We are not victims of all this clutter, congestion, and confusion. We have chosen these things, and now it is time to choose something new. The time has come to re-create.

Listen as I whisper three of the most powerful words in history into your ear. The great artists and scientists knew the power of these words. Allow these three words to permeate every corner of your being and every aspect of your life, and you will live a life of such authenticity that has rarely been witnessed.

Simplify. Simplify. Simplify.

Which parts of your life are confusing, congested, or cluttered? Simplicity is the way to clarity.

Some people argue that they work better in the midst of chaos and confusion or that they feel more at home in the midst of a cluttered environment. I have no doubt that this may be true for some people. But in most cases I find that the organized and simplified way has not been tried and found wanting but rather has not been tried at all.

Give the path of simplicity a chance in your life.

WHY DO WE COMPLICATE THINGS?

We yearn for simplicity, but our lives have a habit of getting out of control, a habit of becoming overwhelmed and overcrowded. Usually we have only ourselves to blame for how complicated our lives have become. Indeed in many ways we seem attracted to the complicated. We complicate our lives for four main reasons: We don't know what we really want, we don't have a clear sense of the purpose of our lives, we are scared of missing out on something, and we want to be distracted from the real challenges of the inner life.

Do you know what you want? I find that most people don't. They know what they don't want. If you ask a single person "What are you looking for in a partner?" they very often answer by saying, "Well, I don't want someone who is insecure or someone who is not spontaneous." If you ask someone what they are looking for in a job, they very often reply, "Oh, I just need to get out of this place. I'll do anything—I just can't do this any longer." We very often answer questions about what we want in the negative. Getting clear about what we want is critical to simplifying our lives. People who know what they want answer in the positive: "I want to be with someone who has a strong sense of self, isn't trying to be someone he isn't, and enjoys spontaneity" or "I'm looking for a position in marketing where I feel my creativity will be celebrated by a team of people I enjoy working with."

We complicate our lives because we don't know what we want.

Do you have a clear sense of what your purpose, your core values, and your critical success factors are? In the corporate setting, these things are talked about all the time. Most companies pull their core values, strategies, and purpose out of the lofty imaginings of some high-level executives, but often they bear no relation to what is really true about the company. Having a clear sense of our core values and critical success factors are most useful when they drive an organization toward its overall purpose, which in general terms is to become the best company it can possibly be.

I think we can also apply this to our lives as individuals. For example, your purpose is to become the-best-version-of-yourself. This purpose gives us the goal, the dream, the big picture. One of your core values may be honesty. If that is the case, you know that no matter what happens, you want that always to be true about you. It is a core value, and core values don't change. Then we have critical success factors. If being a good parent is one of your strategic objectives, then one of your critical success factors might be to spend a lot of time with your children. If one of your strategic objectives over the next twelve months is to get into shape, then your critical success factors in this area may be to work out regularly and eat foods that fuel your body more efficiently. Critical success factors change from time to time as our strategic objectives change. Let me give you an example from the corporate world.

I love the story of Southwest Airlines. Ask yourself what things are true about Southwest Airlines. They have low fares, they are casual and fun, they use only one type of plane, they have the highest on-time record, they don't rely heavily on the hub system but provide point-to-point service, they have no seat assignments and no priority boarding, they have the highest rate of online booking in the industry, they don't use travel agents, they have a high level of customer satisfaction, they offer no first class . . . and so on. Now ask yourself what their three critical success factors are. These are things that a company determines are critical to its success, things it wants always to be true about it. The fact that the company uses only one type of plane plays a role in its success because it allows Southwest to buy parts in bulk, makes repairing and maintaining the aircraft more efficient, and allows Southwest to switch crews from one aircraft to another with maximum efficiency. But it is not one of the company's critical success factors. The three things that it wants always to be true are low fares, timeliness, and customer satisfaction. These are their critical success factors.

A customer asked a Southwest gate agent why the airline didn't have seats in the boarding lines so that people could sit down while they were waiting in line. The agent replied, "The seats would cost money, and then we would have to raise the fares, and we are committed to low fares." The agent was clear about Southwest's critical success factors, which made it easy for her to answer the question. If she was not clear she might spend hours, days, and even weeks thinking about how to get the company to put seats there; she would take the request to her manager. Then if the manager wasn't clear about their critical success factors, she would spend time thinking about it and take it to her supervisor. Purpose brings clarity about what direction we should move in. Core values give clarity to how we will behave as we move in that direction. Critical success factors bring clarity about what we should do to move in that direction.

Southwest was recently offered new routes into San Francisco but turned them down. People said the company was crazy and criticized it, saying that these were valuable routes that could make the airline a lot of money. So why did the company turn them down? San Francisco gets fog. Nobody can control that, and that could affect Southwest's on-time record. Being on time is one of its critical success factors, so it turned the routes down. Knowing who you are and what you do helps bring clarity to your decision making, especially when you are faced with new opportunities.

The CEO of Southwest recently received a letter from a passenger who was complaining that the flight attendants were joking during the safety announcements. The passenger thought that this was taking their relaxed way of doing things too far. Most companies would write back apologizing and enclose a discount voucher or product coupons, but in his letter to the passenger, the CEO wrote, "We will miss you."

Customer service is one of Southwest's strategic anchors, but the customer doesn't get to decide who and what Southwest is and does. Southwest gets to decide that, and it seeks to completely satisfy customers who want what they offer. If you want to fly first class, Southwest is not your airline. People at Southwest know who they are, and that brings clarity to every aspect of their daily operations.

Leaders, visionaries, and geniuses usually have a very clear sense of purpose, and they draw their direction from their purpose. They don't allow their tempers and appetites and impulses to blow them off course or to direct their daily affairs. They allow a deep sense of purpose and conviction to guide their actions and passions. They know what factors are most likely to guarantee their success, and they focus on those factors.

I remember the first time I heard the story about Jesus going into a village and healing all the people who were sick and hurting. The next morning, he woke before dawn and went alone to a quiet place to pray and regain his strength. Later Peter came running to him and said, "Everyone in the village is looking for you." Most people would go down into the village square, allowing themselves to be showered with gifts and praise, basking in their glory. Most people would be shaking hands, kissing babies, and signing autographs. But not Jesus. He had a very clear sense of who he was and the mission before him. So he told Peter and the others, "Let us go to the other villages, so that I may speak there also. It is for this that I have come." Now, that is a statement of purpose and clarity.

Isn't it time you got clear about who you are and what the strategic anchors are in your life? Remember, a strategic anchor is something that you determine is critical for your success, something you want always to be true about you. You don't want to make a list of ten. You probably want only two or three. Together, these two or three anchors should be able to get you through any situation. For example, if you choose honesty as one of your anchors, it will instantly bring clarity to a course of action in the great majority of situations.

Get clear about who you are and who you are not, about what you do and what you don't do. The sooner you get clear on these things, the sooner your life will begin to simplify and flourish because of the clarity that simplicity will bring. We complicate our lives because we don't have a clear sense of what our core values and strategic anchors are.

Another reason we complicate our lives is that we are scared of missing out on something. Our lives often become complicated because we overwhelm our schedules by saying yes to everyone and everything. This is one of the symptoms of not knowing what we want or what our core values and purpose are.

In college I had a roommate who couldn't resist any opportunity for adventure. Paul was a wonderful guy, was caring and thoughtful, and had a great sense of humor, but he couldn't say no to any opportunity. He was constantly spreading himself too thin, and as a result he was often stressed and overwhelmed. One day I asked him why he was like this. In a very honest moment, he told me that he was scared that he was going to miss out on something.

Over the years I have met many people like Paul. Some are this way when it comes to relationships, others are this way when it comes to professional opportunities, others are this way socially, and some, like Paul, cannot resist any chance for an adventure. By getting clear about what we deeply desire and about what our purpose and values are, we become clear about when to say yes and when to say no.

By saying yes to everything, you are almost certainly missing out on the one thing that is intended just for you or on the one person who is intended just for you. How many of us know people who are dating someone just because they like having someone to be with? They know that this person is not the one for them, but they don't want to be alone. Chances are that while they are spending time with this person, they are missing dozens of opportunities to meet the person who is right for them. When you know what you are looking for, you realize that some dates would just be a waste of both people's time and emotional energy.

When you say yes to one thing, you automatically say no to all the other options, even if just for that moment, that day, that week. That is part of the reason we don't get really clear about who we are and what we want, because we like to keep our options open. But options often cloud things. Options often complicate things. We complicate our lives because we are scared of missing out on something.

Another reason we complicate our lives with all this clutter, congestion, and confusion is that we don't want to face the question "What am I here for?" It is a difficult question, not one we can settle in an afternoon sitting around with some trusted friends. Parents, professors, and guidance counselors cannot answer this question for us. It takes time and a variety of experiences, and it requires that we listen vigilantly to our inner voice. Sometimes we don't want to listen to the gentle voice within us, so we drown it out with myriad pleasures and pastimes. In the process, we usually overindulge our tempers, our appetites, and our impulses, placing ourselves farther and farther from the enduring happiness that we deeply yearn for and rendering us less and less able to reach out for it.

We complicate our lives to avoid the real challenges of our inner life. We need to take the time to get clear about these things— purpose, identity, desires, values—so that we can see with great clarity what matters most in our everyday lives. Clarity and simplicity are best friends. Life becomes much simpler as you begin to develop a sense of who you are, what you want, what your values are, and what role you are called to play in the wonderful adventure we call life!

DECISION MAKING

How will you develop this clarity? By simplifying your life, stripping away all that is unnecessary, all that brings clutter, confusion, chaos, and congestion. From that simplicity will emerge all that you are and all that you truly desire for the right reasons.

Life is a series of choices. To make great choices, you must first become very clear about why you are making them. This clarity cannot be obtained in the midst of the noisy, busy world. Clarity cannot be achieved in the midst of personal chaos, whether self-imposed or not. Allow simplicity to direct your life, and permit a measure of silence and solitude to have their proper place in the course of your daily activities. Then you will catch glimpses of the-best-version-of-yourself. This vision will then guide and inspire your decisions and actions.

So much of our unrest and unhappiness comes from not knowing what to do in certain situations or how to decide in particular circumstances or what to choose when certain opportunities arise. Clarity is the great gift that simplicity brings, and clarity in decision making is something to which we should all aspire.

Is there a question that you need to answer? Is there a choice that you need to make? Is there an opportunity that you need to pursue or that you need to turn your back on? Is there a relationship that you need to throw yourself into or walk away from? What is clouding your judgment? Why all the confusion?

One way to get to some clarity is by nakedly examining your motives. Motives provide a window through which we can observe our decisions—and indecision—more closely. Sometimes it may be difficult to establish clarity about what you believe is the right thing to do in a certain situation. At these times motives can be powerful indicators. By looking honestly at the motives that are driving you toward a certain action or repelling you from another course of action, it may be easier for you to determine which direction you should take in the situation at hand.

Our motives can teach us a lot about ourselves. They often reveal what drives us, what we are afraid of, whose opinions impact our decision making, and what we consider important.

It is also important to note that it is very rare that a person has a completely pure motive. Say, for example, that you are walking along and there is an old woman who is in obvious need of someone to help her cross the street in a place where there is no light. You may help her because you feel sorry for her or because you would feel guilty if you didn't. You may help her just to be helpful or because you know you will feel better about yourself if you do. You may help her because a woman you are trying to impress is watching or to be a good example to your little brother and sister. You may just do it out of a sense of obligation. But chances are you will help her for a combination of these reasons. And that's okay. The more we are able to honestly identify those motives, the more insight we will have into the way we make our decisions. All of this knowledge becomes very powerful if we decide we wish to change the way we make decisions.

What people do and what people say is interesting, but *why* people do and say the things they do is absolutely fascinating. Getting to the core of our motives requires a transparency, a humility, and a vulnerability that are as rare as they are difficult to achieve.

Think about your work for a moment. Why do you work as hard as you work? Maybe you work hard and maybe you don't, but the question remains the same. If you work seventy-five hours a week, why do you do that? If you spend a lot of time at work goofing around on the Internet, killing time, why? Examine your motives. Some people work hard because they love what they do. Some people are lazy at work because they don't feel appreciated. Now go deeper into your motives. Who or what drives your work? Some people work for their spouse and children, to support them financially. I think my father was driven in his work by the desire to gives his sons a better life than he had himself. Others are driven by a desire to impress friends, colleagues, or a boss. Some people are driven by a desire for prestige, power, acclaim, money, advancement, and promotions.

Look for a moment at the relationship between parents and children. If you have children, what motives do you have for pushing them in certain directions or discouraging them from certain paths? It seems that children today are involved in a thousand different activities that leave parents running in six directions at once. What motivates this madness? Why do we subscribe to it? Do we have our children's best interests at heart, or are we just trying to fit in? Is it helpful to children to be involved in so many things, or are they doing it just because everyone else is doing it?

Why do you date a certain type of person and not another?

Why do you volunteer?

Why do you avoid certain family members?

Why? Our motives tell us a lot about who we are. If you have a decision to make and you can't find clarity about it, peel back a layer or two of confusion by examining the motives that draw you in one direction or another. Then do the next right thing. Understanding your motives will help you master the moment of decision.

THE ART OF SCHEDULING

Another area of our lives that is desperately in need of being simplified is our schedules. As we are quickly discovering, if we are going to develop a clear sense of purpose, identity, desire, and values, we have to allocate some time to our inner life. Most of us have schedules so overwhelmed with activities and meetings, social commitments, and the unexpected urgent things that we never get around to that much-needed time of silence and solitude to reconnect with an emerging vision of who we truly are.

This is the greatest lesson in simplifying your life: Learn to say no. Many of us really have a hard time with this. For all the reasons that we have discussed, from not wanting to miss out on anything to wanting to please everyone, we really have a hard time saying no.

If your life is overcrowded, it is because you are doing more than it is right for you to do. Seek your role. Being perfectly yourself means doing *only* the things that are intended for you to do. You have to find your place in the grand scheme of life, but you will not find it by busying yourself with a million things that were not intended for you.

If we sense that something is missing, if we yearn for something or someone wonderful in our lives, we must learn to step back from all the frenetic activity. We must create a gap in our lives, a space—yes, those voids that we fear so much. Only then will that special something or that special someone come to inhabit the gap.

Learn to say no. Start to create some space in your life for yourself and for the new things that you want so desperately to come into your life. If someone asks you to do something or invites you somewhere, ask him would it be all right if you got back to him. Write the request down. Expand the moment between event (in this case, the invitation or request) and response (in this case, scheduling). This way you will have time to really think about whether you want to commit that time to that activity. You will have time to examine why you feel drawn to it. Is it because you want to or because you feel it would be good for you or because you feel you must do it?

We do a lot of things because we feel that we must do them. Too often when we ask ourselves, *Why am I doing this?* the answer is because *I must.* But it's not true. We choose to do the things we do. Yes, there are occasions when circumstances are beyond our control, but very often they are the result of an earlier choice. *I must* is sometimes a matter of self-deception. We often imagine that our involvement in that particular activity is absolutely indispensable. Would the world really end if we didn't do it?

I have a note card that I use as a bookmark. It is a very ordinary note card, and on it I have written *Your Life is Your Own*. That statement is true, though I often forget it. Our lives are our own, but so often we get entangled in a web of obligations, most of which are imaginary. Our lives are our own, and we can give them away to whom and what we wish.

We live in a complex world of unlimited opportunity. There are a thousand people and activities competing for every moment of your life. The inner world and the outer world are constantly competing for our attention. The more clarity we can get internally, the more we will thrive externally. But the work of the inner life of reflection requires real attention, and the outer life of activity is extremely seductive.

Often we use activity to distract us from the real questions, from the real work of our lives, from the restlessness and conflicts that are raging within us. But we cannot keep up activities forever, and when we stop to rest and sleep, it is often these questions that make us toss and turn.

The key to thriving in the midst of complexity is simplicity. Scheduling is a practical tool that we use every day; let's start using it to simplify our lives. Just because there is a blank space on your schedule, you don't have to fill it. Otherwise, you can rush around your whole life doing "urgent" things. The problem with that is that the most important things are hardly ever urgent. Maybe it's time you put together a not-to-do list!

MONEY AND THINGS

To a certain point, money and things do simplify our lives, but most of us are well beyond that point, where they add complexity to our lives. I am not saying that money and things are not wonderful or that they are intrinsically bad. I am saying only that we need to be aware of the ways they can affect us and complicate our lives.

There is a great line in the movie *Wall Street.* Gordon Gekko, the legendary investment guru, says to Bud Fox, the youngster looking to make a name for himself, "The thing about money is that it makes you do things you don't want to do." I suspect that at different times in our lives we have all done things we didn't want to do in order to pay the bills. It's a part of life in developed nations. It was a part of life in the agricultural age. It has perhaps always been a part of life. For thousands of years people have been doing things they would rather not do in order to work their way up to doing what they really wanted to do. It's a way of life and contributes to helping us create clarity about who we are, what we are here for, and what is really important to us.

But money has a unique way of clouding our judgment. The money itself is just dirty paper, and what it represents to most people is not just more stuff but also more opportunities. The most devastating poverty after lack of adequate food, water, and shelter is lack of opportunity. Lack of opportunity devastates not the body but also the spirit. The great appeal of money is that it can buy opportunities. Whether those opportunities come in the form of education, travel, or more leisure time, it is usually the imagined opportunity that seduces us, not the money.

Money complicates our lives because once we have it, we have to protect it. For individuals that means bank accounts, investment portfolios, and retirement funds. For nations it means weapons and armies. All of this adds complexity to our lives. Don't get me wrong, I'd rather have the complexity of money than not have any money at all, but it is important to understand how money affects our daily living. With every bank and investment account, there are the monthly statements, which you don't really study, but you glance at them. Sometimes they are up and sometimes they are down. Sometimes you wonder if there is going to be enough money in that account to cover the check you wrote yesterday. All of this requires mental and emotional energy. Yes, emotional energy. We invest a lot of emotional energy in our money.

How can we simplify the financial aspect of our lives? A budget may be one step. Consolidating bank accounts, investment accounts, and retirement accounts is another way if we have multiple accounts. Then, of course, there are the credit cards. How much simpler would your life be if you had only one credit card?

After the money come the things—the stuff we buy because we just have to have it, the stuff we buy because everyone else has one, the stuff we buy because we were having a bad day, and the stuff we buy because we feel like rewarding ourselves. The thing about possessions is that they rent space in our minds. Every thing we have requires mind space, and I probably don't need to point out that mind space is limited, so the more you crowd it, the more confusing things become.

I know a lot of people who own vacation homes in warmer or more exotic parts of the country or the world than where their family homes are. Even those who manage the "living in two places thing" well still have to worry about the other place, all the time. When they are at home they worry about the second home, and when they are at the second home they have to worry about the first home. Is the lawn being mowed? Has it been broken into? Will the hurricane wipe it out? Did we remember to turn the water off at the main? Then there are the bills to pay, and it's not so much a matter of having the money as it is the hassle of actually paying them.

I know, I know—these may seem like the problems of the wealthy to many people. A lot of people would like to sign up for problems like these. I am just using them as an example of how possessions rent space in our minds and complicate our lives.

I read a very powerful line in Richard Foster's work, *Celebration of Discipline*. In it, he discusses the ways possessions can complicate and rule our lives: "Learn to enjoy things without having to own them." It struck me very deeply, because I like having my own things. But it made me realize that sometimes it is more enjoyable to be able to use something for the day or a week, or even a month, and not have to give it permanent space in your mind.

One of the most powerful ways for us to simplify our lives is in the area of money and things. Examining our attitudes toward money and things can also provide valuable insight into how we perceive ourselves, and the motives that drive us.

- Do you buy things because you want them, or do you buy them because you need them?
- Do you evaluate people's success on the basis of possessions and net worth, or on the basis of the goodness of their character and relationships?
- Is your identity closely linked to your money and possessions, or do you draw your identity from who you are and what you are here for?
- Do you shop for leisure, or do you shop only when necessary?
- Are you always buying gadgets that you think are going to save you time?
- Is it hard for you to discard possessions even when you don't

need or use them anymore, or do you find a certain liberation in discarding possessions?

- Do you share your possessions with others? Are you generous with your money?
- Do you buy things because they are useful, or because they
bring you status?
- Do you focus on what you don't have and can't yet afford?
Or are you focused on personal development, relationships,
and all the good things that you do have?
- Do you seek happiness through things, or through making a
contribution to the lives of the people around you?

Next time you go shopping, pick up the item you are thinking
of buying. Hold it in your hands and pause for a moment. Think:
*Do I really need this? How much space is this going to rent in my
mind? Is this really the best use of my money?* There will be times
when you will buy whatever it is. Wonderful. Enjoy it. There will
be other times when you put it down and walk away. Wonderful.
Enjoy the liberation.

Let us also never lose sight of the fact that millions still struggle
just for food to eat and clean water to drink. It seems impossible
that almost two billion people, one-third of the world's popula-
tion, are still without adequate nourishment and healthy water,
but it is true. Three billion people, one-half of the world's popula-
tion, live on less than two dollars a day. The way we live our lives
from a material perspective affects the lives of other people at
home and abroad. There are no personal acts. It is with this in
mind that Mother Teresa suggested, "Live simply, so that others
may simply live."

Things and money have value only inasmuch as we use them
to help us become the-best-version-of-ourselves and to help other

people realize their full potential. The moment they distract us from this, they become our masters and we become their slaves.

PRACTICAL FIRST STEPS

We have covered a lot of ground, and perhaps you feel a little overwhelmed by how overwhelmed you are, or a little overwhelmed by how much simplifying you have just realized that you would really like to do. So where do we start?

I don't know about you, but I like resolutions that are practical, manageable, and measurable. It is amazing how complicated our lives can get and how cluttered our spaces can get. Whether it is your house or apartment, your car or your office, your environments can have a very powerful impact on your peace of mind and the level of happiness you experience. Your environment can also say things to you and about you.

I am an unusually tidy male. Everything is always in the right place. My house is tidy, my office is tidy, and my car is tidy. I don't have knickknacks; they clutter my space and that clutters my mind. If you come to my house and there are things all over the place, you will know that I am sick, unhappy, or confused about something. The inner reality seeks an external expression.

But sometimes tidying up my environments brings inner clarity. So once a year I commit to the great dejunking. It is a process of material liberation. This is the first step I suggest to you in your quest for simplicity and clarity.

I begin by working my way through my house from one room to the next, getting rid of things, things I never use, things I thought I'd use but haven't since last year's dejunking, clothes that don't fit me or are worn out, books that bored me to tears and that I refuse to inflict on another, and any number of other possessions.

I attack one room at a time with great big black garbage bags in hand, but only one room on any one day. I don't want to just do it. I want to learn from it by reflecting on it as I do it. I usually spread it over the course of a couple of weeks, and it is extraordinary how much stuff I collect from year to year. It is also amazing how liberating it can be to get rid of all this unneeded material clutter. At the end of this great dejunking, I take all the black garbage bags filled with my surplus belongings and donate them to a local charity.

Clutter brings confusion. What areas of your life are congested? What areas of your physical world are congested? An environment can have a powerful impact on your inner life. If your environment is congested and cluttered, it is amazing how that can cloud your judgment and decision making. Start simplifying and organizing your environments and see if it doesn't bring some order and clarity to your inner world.

If you get done with that and are still yearning for more clarity about your purpose, identity, desires, and values, unplug your television for a month. Let a bit of peace and quiet into your home. Most people can't do it. It's unnerving how addicted we are to that box. But if you have the self-control to unplug it for a month, you will be amazed how much more peaceful your home will be, how much more in touch with yourself you will become, and how this one change will affect communication in your relationships. It isn't just the absence of the noise; it's the absence of all the fake hype and constant messaging. If it is as powerful for you as it was for me, you may want to really think hard before you plug it in again.

The seventh lesson for enduring happiness is this:

SIMPLIFY.

Simplicity is one of the enduring principles of happiness. For decades, we have added layer on layer of complexity to our lives, all in the name of progress. The issue at hand is no longer basic survival. The real challenge is to find a way to thrive in this complex modern world.

As I look around in my travels, I see an awful lot of people just surviving, just hanging on, or just getting by. I remain convinced that if we are to learn once again to thrive, simplicity is one of our greatest allies. We yearn for simplicity. The more we are willing to simplify, the more the clouds of confusion will begin to lift, the more clearly we will begin to see ourselves for who we are and the world around us for what it is, and the freer we will be.

Simplify. Simplify. Simplify.

Applying the Seventh Lesson for
Enduring Happiness:

SIMPLIFY

I will apply the seventh lesson for enduring happiness
to my life by taking the following steps:

1. I will learn to master the moment of decision. I will remind myself each day that my life is my own, that I can say yes or no to any request or invitation, and that each moment is mine to use as I see fit. I will learn that saying no is a powerful way to simplify my life.

2. I will examine the various aspects of my life—physical, emotional, intellectual, spiritual, professional, and financial—to identify my critical success factors. I will write them down and review them from time to time to assess my progress in each of these areas. I will allow my decisions to be guided by these critical success factors.

3. I will be mindful that money and possessions are useful only inasmuch as they help me and others become the-best-version-of-ourselves. Before I buy something I will ask myself, *Do I really need this, or do I just want this?* I will make myself free to answer this question honestly by reminding myself that it is okay to want things that I do not need. But in each case, if it is something that I do not genuinely need, I want to be sure that I am not being driven by compulsion, that I am in fact free not to have it.

4. I will unplug my television for one month. During this time I will examine the way I feel, how the energy changes in my home, and how my relationships are affected by the absence of this noise and messaging. Instead of watching television, I will read more and spend more time simply talking to the people I love, whether in person or on the phone. At the end of this one-month abstinence, I will seriously consider the effects television has on my life and relationships before plugging it back in. If I do decide to return to a lifestyle that includes television, I will guard against its negative effects by limiting my exposure and carefully discerning what programs I expose myself to.

5. I will begin the great dejunking of my living and working environments. I will overhaul one room or space at a time, discarding all items that have outlived their usefulness in my life: things I never use, clothes I never wear, and anything that unnecessarily adds to the clutter and congestion of my living and working spaces. Wherever possible I will see to it that my excess belongings are passed on to somebody who needs them.

Eight

What Is Your Mission?

A few weeks ago I went to get my hair cut. My stylist usually likes to bring me up to date on what people have been saying about me. It is quite amusing, and while the stories are almost never true, they usually do spring from some obscure and insignificant fact. For example, one Friday afternoon I went to a jeweler to buy a watch as a birthday gift for my brother Hamish. While they were wrapping the watch, I wandered around the store. Someone must have seen me passing by the diamond rings, because the following Monday my office had eleven calls asking if I was engaged.

On this particular day my stylist didn't have any gossip to report, but she did relay this interesting story. "One of my clients came in the other day and said, 'I heard that you cut Matthew Kelly's hair. Tell that young man that he needs to write a book for people like me. I mean, I'm sixty, but I'm not dead.' "

It struck me immediately because the woman had put her finger on a sentiment that is growing among the people of her demographic. There are many people who are retired or are about to retire—and many who are well before retirement age—who want to continue to live in a way that engages them, challenges them, and allows them to make a difference. This generation of retirees is not going to go off to leisureland to play golf and drink martinis. They want more. They want to stay involved. They want to continue to make meaningful contributions. For some, this means semi-retirement, a lessening of the load. For others it means volunteering or part-time work in a new career altogether. For still others it means learning new skills or finally doing that thing they never had a chance to do when they were younger. Regardless of how it manifests, all of this is evidence of a real yearning that people of all ages are identifying more and more. We want to live more meaningful lives, and we want to make a contribution.

Earlier I mentioned the shifting trends in the workforce, in particular a desire for meaningful work. Seventy percent of American workers wish they had more meaningful work. People want to make a contribution. They don't just want to be another cog in the global economic wheel.

At the other end of the age spectrum, young people seem increasingly unable to even get their minds around the insanity of spending 86,400 hours doing something that they are not passionate about and does little other than increase the wealth of shareholders. Why are so many people in their teens and twenties, and even in their thirties, disillusioned about their futures? Why do they seem to demonstrate so little motivation and drive toward building their futures? Some may say simply because they are young, but I would argue that it is because we have failed to demonstrate to them how they can passionately contribute to society and humanity.

Isn't one of our greatest obligations to help young people, indeed all people, find a way to make a contribution by exercising their unique talents and abilities?

In a variety of cultural, political, corporate, and humanitarian situations, we are failing to connect people of all ages with their unique abilities and with the real needs of other people and worthy institutions. The explosion of passion and purpose takes place when unique abilities and needs meet. We are failing to create this explosion in all too many people's lives. Certainly we are each responsible for finding a way to express our unique abilities. It would be a mistake to abdicate that responsibility. But we also have a collective responsibility to create a framework that gives more and more people the opportunity to do so.

My grandfather's generation was driven by the quest to survive. Survival was the most compelling aspect of their lives. I am not sure they thought much about the quest for happiness. The idea of searching for happiness has emerged relatively late in history and would have been considered by many generations past as a surprising luxury, I suspect. I also wonder if any great number of people in generations past allowed themselves to get bogged down in the idea that they were unhappy. That seems to me to be a leisure pursuit.

My father's generation sought to give their children a better life than they themselves had enjoyed. They found meaning in providing for their families and giving their children the opportunities that they thought were necessary to build a richer, more abundant future, particularly in the area of education. But now, with so many of our basic needs and wants taken care of, a universal desire is emerging among people of all ages: to live more meaningful lives. This desire is the beginning of a cultural revolution. This hunger to live more meaningful lives will perhaps change the face of business and politics more than any other idea has for decades. It will certainly change the way we live our lives as individuals.

So where do we turn to find this meaning?

In the natural order of human progression, sociologists and

philosophers talk generally about three stages. The first stage is the struggle for *survival*. This was my grandfather's struggle. We see this stage clearly in the lives of individuals, but we also see it in the lives of nations. There are a great many developing nations still almost completely absorbed in the struggle for survival, and there are a great many people in advanced nations living paycheck to paycheck necessarily obsessed with this stage.

In the next stage, we begin to acquire certain types of knowledge along with an understanding of processes and systems in a quest for *independence*.

As we acquire specialized knowledge and grow to understand how certain systems work, we begin to thrive both socially and professionally. It is usually at this point that we focus on becoming more and more *effective* at whatever it is we are doing. This is the famous quest for effectiveness, and is usually described as the third stage. But I would argue that it is the fourth.

The reality is that most people miss a stage. To be truly effective, you have to be doing the right thing. It doesn't matter how quickly or proficiently you are able to do the wrong thing or how many hours a day or how many years of your life you give to doing the wrong thing; it's still the wrong thing. Doing the wrong thing well doesn't make it the right thing. I am not speaking of right and wrong in the moral sense but rather in the sense of what a person is best suited to and for. I think we can agree that for Picasso to have spent his life as a pilot would have been the wrong thing for Picasso, and that if Francis of Assisi had taken over his father's trading business, it would have been the wrong thing for Francis, and that for Albert Einstein to have spent his life as a high school science teacher would have been the wrong thing for him. There is nothing wrong with being a pilot or a business owner or a high school teacher if this is what you are called to.

So if stage 1 is survival and stage 2 is independence, effectiveness and thriving are actually stage 4. What is stage 3? Stage 3 is *mission*. Most people miss it, and that is why most people lead lives of quiet desperation.

The happiest people I know are people who have a sense of mission. They have a joy that nobody can take away from them. The joy of their lives is linked not to the worldly scope or scale of the mission but to the belief that they are uniquely suited to that role and the conviction that they have been called to it. They have a sense that they are in the right place at the right time doing the right thing. Their lives make sense to them. They may not make sense to the people around them, even some of the people closest to them. But their lives make sense to them. Does your life make sense to you? Are you at peace with who you are, where you are, and what you are doing?

People who have a sense of mission in their lives are filled with a joy that is independent of substance and circumstances. Even in the middle of tremendous trials, they still have an enormous capacity for joy. The reason is that whatever they are enduring, they know that it is not for naught. They serve a purpose higher than their own gratification.

For the most part, their missions are usually fairly simple and humble. They are not out trying to cancel Third World debt or overturn laws in more than a hundred nations that still treat women abominably. A handful of people *are* called to these great missions, but most of us are called to missions more manageable in the context of our daily lives. That's the thing about a mission. You don't choose a mission; you are sent on a mission. This is why so many explanations of the different stages of human development skip straight over the mission stage. It proposes a problem in a society that idolizes self-determination. If these happy people have the conviction that they have been called to their mission, who called them? If you don't choose a mission but rather are called to and sent on a mission, who does the sending?

According to fifty years of opinion polls conducted by the Gallup Organization, ninety-four percent of us believe in God, ninety percent of us pray, and eighty-eight percent of us believe that God loves us. Who does the calling and the sending? God. Of course we couldn't talk about it in public schools, and maybe that's why we drop the third stage. But is there any point in being really effective at the wrong things, and isn't it a little depressing to think of millions of people spending their whole lives doing things that are contrary to their unique abilities and purpose? So whether we can talk about God and mission in public high schools is not the point. The point is that people need to be made aware of the role mission plays in our lives.

Finally, before we begin our discussion of exactly how we can go about finding our mission in life and helping others to do the same, I would like to point out that mission and spirituality are inseparably linked. I don't know anybody who is experiencing enduring happiness who does not have some sense of mission in his or her life. In fact, it seems the stronger the sense of mission a person has, the greater his or her capacity for enduring happiness. But the actual mission is an external expression of an internal reality. I don't know anybody who is happy who doesn't have a spiritual perspective or outlook. Finding your mission in life and developing your spirituality are intrinsically linked.

We yearn for more meaning in our lives; we are hungry to make a contribution and are plagued by the feeling that we are out of place. All of this is because we have simply failed to seek and find our mission. Mission is the something you are best suited for, something you are called to and created for. If you can stay open to the possibility of such an idea, then you are about to experience a whole new level of life.

What is your mission in life? Let's begin to unveil it.

FINDING YOUR MISSION

We all long to make sense of life, to understand its purpose, and indeed, our purpose. We have already established that our purpose is to become the-best-version-of-ourselves. But once we set ourselves to this purpose in earnest, we very quickly discover that we cannot become our best selves without helping others to do the same. The two are inseparably intertwined. And not only that but we also want to play a unique role. We yearn for the passion and enthusiasm that comes from our own specific mission.

What is your mission in life? Take a few minutes to write down whatever comes to mind. It doesn't have to be one thing. It may be many things. Some will be more important than others, but write them all down, both large and small roles.

At my seminars I have often asked, "What is your mission in life?" Some of the responses I've gotten are "to raise my children"; "to take care of my family"; "to leave the world better than I found it"; "to be a good person"; "to serve God"; "to be a good doctor"; "to live life to the fullest." These are the quick answers. But the question requires serious consideration. I don't have the answer to give you. Your parents cannot give it to you, though they dearly wish that they could. Your friends cannot tell you what your mission in life is. You will not discover it on TV. Nor can teachers, coaches, professors, mentors, preachers, priests, or rabbis give you the answer to this question. They *can* help by making suggestions and pointing out what they see from their vantage point. And yet, when all of these have weighed in, it still is a question you must answer for yourself. Finding your mission in life is a deeply personal quest.

Finding our mission is possible only if we are willing to look beyond our self. Mission is not driven by our own desire to do something, be something, or have something, though certainly that desire may play a role. It is driven by the needs of others and the needs of the world. Mission is a meeting between self and service. If we are genuinely in search of mission, our desire must be to serve as we are needed and where we are needed. Mission is driven by need—the needs of others and our need to serve. At the same time, I believe that our missions have been designed to correspond with our deepest desires and our unique talents. Mission is where our talents and passions collide with the needs of others and the world. If we are unable to see ourselves as being called by God to mission, then let us be called by the needs of others and the needs of our wonderful but wounded world. Frederick Buechner, a minister and author, observed that mission "is the place where your deep gladness meets the world's deep need."

The thing about our mission is that it is not about us, and yet, you will quickly discover that the paradox of mission is that it is the source of our greatest happiness. Once we have discovered our mission and set ourselves to it, the challenge is to keep mission focused on service. However great the service we may render, however great our contribution, we must avoid the temptation to let it become about us. Mission saves us from our self-centered living and delivers us to a sustainable happiness by averting our gaze from self to others.

It is also important to recognize from the outset that our mission may change at different times in our lives. A mother's role in raising a child is a perfect example. This mission has many stages, from carrying the child in the womb and delivery to the early weeks of infancy, and from adolescence to adulthood. At each stage a mother nurtures a child in different ways. In the mission of motherhood, the mission remains the same but requires different approaches depending on the stage.

There are other examples where our mission may change altogether. A young person may feel called to the Peace Corps in his or her early adulthood. They may spend a couple of years in this commitment and then move on to marry, raise a family, and pursue some other professional calling. The Peace Corps mission in this case is a temporary one. A mission doesn't have to be lifelong. Many are temporary and usually prepare us, in ways unknown to us at the time, for some future mission.

The trouble is in the knowing. How do we know when we have discovered our mission? How do we know if it is a temporary mission or a lifelong mission? The answer is that it is complicated. And as with all things complicated, it helps to begin by working from the general to the specific—from what applies to everyone to what applies to you specifically.

In the broadest terms, our mission is to become the-best-version-of-ourselves. We live this mission moment by moment, by making choices that lead us to celebrate and defend our best selves. It requires a proactive offensive and defensive effort. Choosing to exercise is an offensive action, while deciding not to spend time with a certain person who leads you away from your best self is a defensive act. We are all here to become the-best-version-of-ourselves. So this is the first part of your mission. It is not uniquely yours—you share this part of your mission with every person in the human race—but you personalize it by the way you live it out.

As we move one step closer to our specific mission, we next discover that our mission is to do what we can, where we can, how we can, right now, to make the world a better place. The reason many people never find their specific and unique mission is because they never take the general aspects of their mission seriously.

Our greatest strength as human beings is our ability to make a difference in the lives of other people, and yet it is the most unemployed of all human abilities. If we wish in earnest to discover that part of our mission that is uniquely our own, we must first begin to exercise this great talent. Francis of Assisi encouraged his listeners in this way: "First do what is necessary, then do what is possible, and before long you will find yourself doing the impossible." In our quest for mission, we cannot avoid or neglect the general. If we try this path, the specific will elude us. We are all here to make the world a better place. This is the second part of your mission. Again, it is not uniquely yours—it is part of humanity's shared mission, but you personalize it by the way you live it out.

The more we set ourselves to these first two parts of our mission, the clearer our specific and unique mission will become. Applying ourselves to the general aspects of our mission becomes the means to discovering that part of our mission that is intended just for us. This aspect of your mission is uniquely yours. It will be left undone in history if you do not discover it, embrace it, and fulfill it.

This third and personal part of mission involves you exercising your talents and abilities in a way that only you are capable of, in a place and time that most needs you. This is your personal mission. Only my mother and father could have raised me in the way that I needed to be raised. It was part of their specific mission. There are people at this time in history who need the ideas that I speak and write about. Speaking and writing are part of my specific mission.

Your unique mission may involve raising a child, becoming the president of your nation, or loving your spouse with all your heart. You may be here to make an enormous contribution to the arts or to make a scientific discovery that changes the course of history. You may be here to teach third grade at your local elementary school. The worldly scope and scale of your unique mission is irrelevant; what matters is that you embrace the role that is especially suited to you. Many people turn their backs on their unique mission because it doesn't seem spectacular enough to them or because it doesn't make them enough money. They spend the rest of their lives haunted by the nagging sense that something is wrong or missing.

How do we find our mission? By using the moments of each day to become the-best-version-of-ourselves, by doing all the good things we feel inspired to do where we are right now, by investigating and developing our unique talents and deepest desires, and by listening to the voice of God in our lives. If we earnestly apply ourselves in these ways, our unique mission will gradually reveal itself.

Each of us must find our purpose and place in this world. Peace Pilgrim discussed it this way:

> There is something unique to every human life because every one of us has a *special place in the Life Pattern.* If you do not yet know clearly where you fit, I suggest that you try seeking it in receptive silence. I used to walk amid the beauties of nature, just receptive and silent, and wonderful insights would come to me. You begin to do your part in the Life Pattern by doing all the good things you feel motivated toward, even though they are just little good things at first. You give these priority in your life over all the superficial things that customarily clutter human lives.

We know what we should be doing with our lives more often than we admit. It is one thing not to do something because we do not know that we should be doing it. But to know and not to do is a greater tragedy and causes the human spirit to atrophy. I meet people every day who feel called to do some good thing and they know what it is, but they ignore that calling. When they talk to me about whatever it is they feel called to do, they get animated—their eyes light up and their whole posture and disposition changes. But when I ask them why they don't do it, they become deflated. It always comes down to the fact that they feel trapped by money or the expectations of others, but mostly by the fear of uncertainty. These are real obstacles that can be overcome only with the virtues of courage, fortitude, and perseverance. It will not be easy, but consider the alternative. To know your mission and not to follow it is one of the greatest of human miseries.

The mystery of our mission is revealed to us little by little. This revelation unfolds as we apply what we know to be good and true to our lives. If you do not use the information that has already been revealed to you, the universe will not reveal any more. Step toward your mission, and the next step will become illuminated. Begin today. You can start by doing some good thing that you feel motivated to do. Any good thing will do. With each passing day, apply yourself to the task of doing the good things you are capable of and feel called to, and your heart and mind will begin to fill with a renewed joy and passion for life. Allow yourself to be patiently led from the general to the specific. In time, you will begin to see your unique mission beginning to emerge. Embrace it and celebrate it. George Bernard Shaw, the Irish dramatist, wrote, "This is the true joy in life, the being used for a purpose recognized by yourself as a mighty one."

FINDING YOURSELF

I grew up in a suburb of Sydney, Australia, and my childhood was filled with wonderful memories, but there are a few experiences that stand out, not because they were fun but because they helped to form my view of the world. When I was seventeen, Justin, a family friend, called me one day and asked me if I could spare him a couple of hours on Sunday afternoon. He didn't live very far from us, and the following Sunday I stopped by as I agreed I would.

We began walking down the street from his house, and he explained that we were going to visit some friends of his. We walked about two miles to the next suburb and arrived at a nursing home. Going inside, he went to the nurses' station, and I overheard him explaining to one of the nurses that we had come to visit with some of the old people who didn't get visitors too often. The nurse looked at him a bit suspiciously but pointed him toward one of the wings of the nursing home anyway.

Justin then took a box of chocolates from his coat pocket, and we went into one of the rooms. In the room there were four beds and four men. We said hello and began to pass around the chocolates. One man was keen to start up a conversation; the others looked on suspiciously.

We moved from room to room, spending ten or fifteen minutes in each room. We would pass out chocolates and talk to the old people. Many had not had a visitor in months, and they all had stories about their lives and where they had come from. Sometimes it was hard to strike up a conversation, but in most cases it didn't take much more than to ask, "Where are you from?"

I felt awkward and uncomfortable. The time passed painfully slowly, and I couldn't wait for it to end. Finally it did.

On the way home, Justin explained how lonely some of these people were and how society had abandoned them. Our visit had made this evident. "Do you go there often?" I asked him. He explained that he had never been to that particular nursing home, but that from time to time he tries to visit a different nursing home.

The following week, he called and asked if I would like to join him again. I said I was busy. The week after that, he called again. I told him I had other commitments. He kept calling, and eventually I gave in. This time I was more comfortable with the old people. I started to ask them questions. Justin kept calling, and most weeks I would make up an excuse, but sometimes I would agree to go with him. Over the next several months, we visited a number of nursing homes in the area, and I was exposed to the great need of the elderly in our community. I cannot remember how the transition took place, but over time I found myself going on my own. From time to time, I would try to drag one of my friends along, but most of them resisted and those who did agree to come came only once.

I made friends with some of the old people, and they began to tell me their stories. This was an education that money could not buy, and their stories began to stir deep within me. Careers and wars, raising families and losing families, sickness and health, love and loss, wealth and poverty, adventure and routine, these men and women had experienced everything, and they were more than willing to share it all with me. In fact they needed to tell their stories, and as they did so, their faces began to beam and their eyes began to sparkle.

These men and women had an enormous influence on my life. I can't say that I ever really enjoyed those visits. I had to force myself to go, but I knew that they were drawing me out of my tiny world of self and into a world of others. I never got over being nervous and scared going into those places, but I forced myself to do it, and it built in me a courage that would come in handy as I traveled the world in the years that followed. Though I didn't enjoy going to those nursing homes, I always felt good about myself when I was done with my visits. I would walk home with a joy that didn't come from anything else I could have spent that time doing. Today I know that those nursing-home visits were teaching me and forming me in so many ways that I was unaware of at the time. Most important, they were instructing me about the power of service in the quest to discover who we truly are and what we are here for. In our own place, in our own way, we all have an infinite number of opportunities to serve. It is all too easy to get caught up in our own little world. Service draws us out of our sometimes all-consuming obsession with ourselves and opens us up to the world of others.

There is another story I would like to share with you from the suburbs of Sydney. Shortly before Christmas in 1922, five Australian businessmen were returning from a trip to the Blue Mountains. They debated whether *everyone* was enjoying the Christmas spirit. One of the men asked the others if they were aware of the poverty and need that surrounded the areas where they each owned factories. The other four were surprised to hear of it, and a couple couldn't be convinced of it. The man who raised the subject then challenged the others to investigate his claim a little, and they all agreed to meet at a pub a week later to have a beer and discuss what they discovered.

The other four men were amazed at the number of disadvantaged children and families they found, not in some foreign country but almost in their very backyards. When the group met a week later, the men unanimously agreed that they had to do something about it. They decided that at the very least, every child should be able to join in the spirit of Christmas. So they started at the local orphanages where children were without the love of families and showered them with gifts and candy.

While the men were delivering the food and gifts, the woman in charge of the orphanage asked them their names so that the children could write letters of thanks. Wanting to remain anonymous, one of the men replied, "Er . . . Smith!"

"What about the others?" asked the matron.

"They're Smiths too!" replied the man "We're all Smiths. The Smith Family."

Today The Smith Family is one of Australia's leading charitable organizations, and the five founders have managed to remain anonymous. Over the past eighty years, the organization has continued to review the needs of disadvantaged children and families and responded accordingly.

During the Depression of the late 1920s and early 1930s, The Smith Family assisted with food and clothing for thousands of men, women, and children as unemployment soared. In 1933, when rheumatic fever became a major health issue affecting children, The Smith Family set up a special hospital to care for them. The 1970s saw The Smith Family react to the needs of refugee families fleeing war in Vietnam and Timor and supporting the residents of Darwin, Australia, as they recovered from the devastation of Cyclone Tracy. Throughout the 1970s and 1980s, The Smith Family was spending more than ever on direct financial relief, in many cases to families they had been supporting for generations. Turning to their emergency help clients, they asked them how they could help to put an end to intergenerational disadvantage. They replied, "Help us help our children to get an education." In 2006, more than 23,500 students across Australia were to receive education scholarships from The Smith Family.

Did those five men ever imagine that this is what they would trigger? I suspect not. They did what they could, when they could, where they were. John Wesley wrote, "Do all the good you can, by all the means you can." Most people are astounded by what they are capable of once they start to take the first two parts of their mission seriously. By striving to be our best selves and trying to proactively make the world a better place, most people can have a huge positive influence.

Amazing things begin to happen when we do what we can where we are. Each of us must find a way to serve. I try wherever possible to avoid using the word *must* when I am writing, but I use it emphatically here. Albert Schweitzer, the French medical missionary and Nobel Peace Prize recipient of 1953, expressed the same idea: "I am certain of one thing. The only ones among us who will ever be truly happy are those of us who have sought and found a way to serve."

The greatest shift in most of our lives will take place when we decide to make ourselves radically available to serve. The moment that the internal dialogue moves from the question "What's in it for me?" to the question "How can I serve?" we begin to rapidly move in the direction of discovering our mission in life. Until this shift takes place, it is impossible to embrace our mission, and so the universe will almost certainly keep it hidden from us.

I have a friend in New York who is among the busiest people I know. He has his own television and radio shows, writes books, and supports numerous charities by getting directly involved. Add to this his commitments to his family and friends and the constant social demands of his profession, and you have yourself a very busy man. I have known him for ten years now, and whenever I talk to him on the phone or see him in person, our time together never ends without his asking, "What can I do to help?"

At first I thought he was just being polite, but over time as I have come to know him and the way he lives his life, I have learned that he lives to serve others. He has taught me to keep perspective on my own role and responsibility as a leader. He has planted the question in my mind and into my conversations with others. I now approach people while asking myself, *What can I do to help this person?* And I recommend that you also add the question to your inner dialogue. In your day-to-day happenings, begin to ask yourself how you can help the people who cross your path or how you can serve in the situations presented to you.

Some Eastern traditions refer to the law of dharma. *Dharma* is a Sanskrit word that means "purpose in life." The law of dharma suggests that each and every human being takes physical form to fulfill a unique purpose. It is believed that we arrive at this purpose by focusing on what we are here to give.

The surest way to find yourself is not to take some exotic trip to a distant land. Stay just where you are. You are exactly where you are right now for a reason. Discover that reason before you move on to new pastures. And service is the surest way to discover that reason. Service provides the most direct route to establishing a clear sense of who you are and what you are here for. By shifting our focus from what we can get to what we can give, we open ourselves up to a life of service. The universe will freely reveal your mission once it perceives that you have made yourself available to serve.

Whom will you serve? Some people spend their whole lives serving themselves, their petty interests, and selfish desires. You can measure the greatness of a life by what and whom it serves. Service is essential if you earnestly seek enduring happiness. People and thinkers from almost every philosophical perspective seem to agree on this single truth:

> Service is the rent we pay to be living. It is the very purpose of life and not something you do in your spare time.
>
> —MARIAN WRIGHT EDELMAN

> A generous heart, kind speech, and a life of service and compassion are the things which renew humanity.
>
> —BUDDHA

I know of no great men except those who have rendered great service to the human race.

—VOLTAIRE

Everyone can be great because anyone can serve. You don't have to have a college degree to serve. You don't even have to make your subject and your verb agree to serve . . .

—MARTIN LUTHER KING JR.

The more you serve others, the more fulfilled your life will be.

—DR. BERNIE SIEGEL

Everyone has a purpose in life beyond one's immediate interests and gratifications, though that purpose frequently goes undiscovered.

—JOHN MARKS TEMPLETON

The highest destiny of the individual is to serve.

—ALBERT EINSTEIN

DEVELOPING A HEALTHY SENSE OF SELF

To turn our backs on a life of service is to turn our backs on our very selves. Service is at the very core of our identity as human beings, and to neglect our ability to be of service to others is one of the surest ways to misery and quiet desperation. We see this no more vividly demonstrated than by so many young people in today's culture.

I have noticed that among young people today we are unconsciously promoting a self-centeredness that can absolutely paralyze the human spirit. What I am about to describe is *not true* of *all* young people, and of course there are varying degrees, but it applies to enough that we should begin to question some of our assumptions.

When children are born, we nurture and protect them and dote over them. This of course is natural because they are helpless and need us to do this for them. But as they grow older, we indulge them and spoil them. We constantly tell them how cute they are. We buy them what they want so that they won't cause a scene and often allow them to get away with poor behavior. Perhaps it is that we feel guilty because we don't spend enough time with them. Maybe we just don't have the energy. Or perhaps we remember an upbringing that seemed overly strict. But the result is that we are depriving our children by missing these sometimes small but valuable opportunities to instill character in their young selves. Before you know it, they are going through puberty and the hormones are raging. This seems an even more challenging time, and there are moments when all we want is to keep the peace, so we tolerate outbursts and other behaviors that we would not normally tolerate. We give them their space and tell ourselves that it is just a phase. Now they are in high school, and we tell them to concentrate on their schoolwork so that they can get into a good college. They exploit this in whatever ways they can—let's face it, you and I would too—so they explain that they are under pressure with their schoolwork and other commitments, and we buy it, giving them more liberty and fewer responsibilities within the context of family and community. Finally we send them off to college. By now they have been well and truly indoctrinated with the cultural philosophy that "you will never have four years like this ever again in your life, so enjoy them. This is your time to have fun, don't waste it." Some use this time wisely, but so many others do not, and sooner or later most of them graduate. But they have been trained to focus on themselves. We have trained them. So we shouldn't be surprised if they seem at times to be self-interested, self-absorbed, and unable to recognize the needs of others because they are generally consumed with themselves.

At the same time, we hear educators, parents, and guidance counselors continue to announce that young people are suffering from ever-decreasing levels of self-esteem. Why? What is it that will make young people feel really good about themselves? It isn't designer-label clothing and vacationing in all the right places every year. It doesn't even come from excelling at exams or achieving in the sporting arena. Confidence may come from these things, but self-esteem and confidence are not the same thing. So what is the source of self-esteem?

Having self-esteem and making a contribution are directly linked to each other. We put so much energy into what our children wear and what they achieve but so little energy by comparison into helping them understand who they are and why they really matter. We seem obsessed with helping them to fit in and virtually neglect their real and legitimate need to be comfortable in their own company.

We have betrayed our young people by not instilling in them an understanding of the importance of service in the equation of human happiness. We have not taught them to serve. We have trained them to focus on what they can get rather than what they are here to give. The only valid reason I can find for this error is that we have lost sight ourselves of the enormous role that service plays in a life of enduring happiness. But in truth it probably comes down to practical constraints, such as the fact that in most families today, both parents work.

Too often as a society we focus on what personal advantage we can gain from a situation. Too often the rights of the individual are celebrated at the expense of the common good. Too often we advocate self-determinism and overlook the fact that our destinies are linked. Too often we allow self-interest to rule our hearts, minds, and spirits and overlook the needs of the people that surround us.

The eighth lesson for enduring happiness is this:

FOCUS ON WHAT YOU ARE HERE TO GIVE.

Focusing on what we are here to give is the path to discovering our mission in life and gaining a healthy self-esteem.

When I was a child, my parents taught me that I should never go to anyone's home without bringing them a gift. But this is a lesson of life, not of etiquette. Flowers or a bottle of wine are customary choices for etiquette, but a compliment and a prayer are also gifts in life. Every time we encounter a person, we should give them a gift. Our gifts do not need to be purchased at great cost. In fact, the best gifts are those that are not purchased at all. Perhaps we can give a kind word of encouragement or simply wish them well in their day. In this very real, repetitive, and practical way, we begin to teach ourselves to focus on what we are here to give.

In the quiet moments, when we are alone with nothing but our thoughts and memories, we all need to be able to feel good about ourselves, whether we are young or old. It is the responsibility of each of us individually to do whatever is necessary to feel good about one's self in these quiet moments. It is this audience of one that we must convince that we are using our lives in a worthy way. You have to be able to look yourself in the eye when you gaze into the mirror and really like yourself. Notice that I didn't say you have to be able to look at *yourself* in the mirror. There is often going to be something you don't like or would like to change about your physical appearance, but you have to be able to look yourself in the eye and like who you are.

Self-esteem is essential to enduring happiness. Service is the surest way to build a healthy sense of self, but we must be discerning about who and what we serve. This discernment comes from applying all nine lessons for enduring happiness to our lives. If one lesson is isolated rather than helping us become the-best-version-of-ourselves, the overemphasis can lead to a distortion of our character. Focusing on what we are here to give is one way to build self-esteem and lasting happiness in our lives, but it is only one of nine. Let us revisit for a moment the lessons thus far:

1. Celebrate your progress.
2. Just do the next right thing.
3. Put character first.
4. Find what you love and do it.
5. Live what you believe.
6. Be disciplined.
7. Simplify.
8. Focus on what you are here to give.

Each of these lessons, when applied to the practical moments and decisions in your life, will help you to develop a healthy and well-balanced sense of self. Over time, as you begin to live the lessons of enduring happiness, you will learn to see the good and the bad, the strong and the weak, the willing and the unwilling sides of yourself. And as you mature as a person, you will help others to see and live the lessons also. In fact, the more you teach others to live the lessons, the more you will be able to apply them to your own life. And so it is, even in living the lessons, that the best result is found not when we focus on ourselves but when we turn our gentle gaze toward others and ask ourselves, *How can I help this person become his or her best self?*

Helen Keller observed, "Many people have a wrong idea of what constitutes true happiness. It is not attained through self-gratification, but through fidelity to a worthy purpose." And while we wait for that worthy purpose to reveal itself, let us find a way to serve where we are right now. Service will coax our mission to reveal itself as nothing else can.

Contribute or perish—this is one of the fundamental and guiding principles of the universe. We observe it in a thousand ways in nature, and we witness it in the lives of people. The question we must all ask ourselves is this: What will my contribution be?

Finding our mission in this life is at once simple and complicated. It requires that we both start immediately and wait patiently. It is simple because with a few moments of reflection we can all discover things we can do today that will help us become more perfectly ourselves. It is simple because the needs of other people are often self-evident, and our ability to help them in their need is enormous. But it is also complicated because there is so much need and we cannot attend to it all. It is complicated because we sense that we have a particular role to play. Begin today by doing what you can with what you have, wherever you find yourself. Focus on what you are here to give, and in time your unique mission will reveal itself to you.

Applying the Eighth Lesson for
Enduring Happiness:

FOCUS ON WHAT YOU ARE HERE TO GIVE

I will apply the eighth lesson for enduring happiness
to my life by taking the following steps:

1. I will proactively seek out my mission in life in these four ways: by choosing the-best-version-of-myself in each moment, by doing what I can where I am right now to help others celebrate their best selves and to make the world a better place, by exploring how my talents and passions can be put to use to serve the needs of others, and by listening to the voice of God in my life.

2. I will be mindful of the needs of others both in my local community and in places that I will never visit. I will use a portion of my time, talent, and treasure to serve the needs of others and alleviate suffering in this world.

3. I will develop a healthy sense of self by engaging my greatest talent—my ability to be the difference that makes the difference in the lives of other people. I will remind myself that each opportunity to serve is also an opportunity to grow in virtue. At the same time I will be careful not to lose myself in the insatiable needs of others and be sure to make time for my own legitimate needs—physically, emotionally, intellectually, and spiritually.

4. I will focus on what I am here to give by switching my attention from the question "What's in it for me?" to the question "How can I serve?" Each morning while I am showering or making my way to work I will ask myself, "Whose day can I make today?"

Nine

Why Worry?

When I was a teenager, my room was just down the hallway from my older brother Andrew's room. For his thirteenth birthday, he got a stereo that was capable of making more noise than all the other appliances in the house put together, and as an assertion of his status as oldest brother in the house, he used to blast his music for all to hear, or suffer. One of his favorite bands was the British group Dire Straits. He used to play the *Brothers in Arms* album over and over again. At the time I didn't care for Dire Straits at all, but years later when I started traveling, I found myself humming some of the songs to myself. And one day I found myself buying that very album in an airport music store. I bring all this up because the last song on the album is *"Why Worry."* And worry is the final obstacle to enduring happiness. The song speaks about the inevitability of problems in our lives and troubles in our world. It also reminds us of the hope that brings us through dark times. There will be laughter after pain; there will be sunshine after rain. It has always been this way, so why do we spend so much of our time and energy consumed with worry?

The Things We Worry About

Set this book down and take a few minutes to make a list of all the things you have worried about in your life. Just start writing— the things you worried about as a child, in high school and college, in relationships, professionally and financially, in relation to health and well-being, in relation to the people you love. Also include the things you worry about in relation to finding that tender balance between accepting yourself for who you are and challenging yourself to be all you are capable of being. Write them all down. They don't have to be in any particular order; just start writing.

We worry about a lot of things, don't we? I know I do. Some nights I lie in bed and my mind is just racing with things I need to do, or things I need to tell others about. Then I will begin to construct different scenarios for how a certain situation is going to work out. And because, as I previously admitted, I can tend toward the negative, before you know it I will have worked myself into a real state. I have to stop, consciously, and remind myself that I am imagining all these scenarios, that they are not real. I do this by reminding myself that in the past situations have never worked out the way I thought they would.

I don't know if you have noticed, but things very, very rarely work out the way we think they will. And the way we think things will work out is the major source of our worry. So why worry? The reason, of course, is that we want to be in control. Worry creates the illusion that we have some element of control. Worry doesn't solve anything, but by worrying we convince ourselves that we are doing something about a situation that is entirely out of our control. The reality is that we usually have little or no control over the things we worry about. If we had control over them, we would act. It is not being able to act that usually causes us to worry.

Worry is a self-deception. Worry is often born from our un-willingness to admit that we are powerless over a certain situation or circumstance.

But telling people not to worry is like telling them not to think of a white elephant. How often I hear people say, "Worrying won't help" or "Worrying is not going to change anything." As true as these words are, they don't empower people to turn around and say, "You're absolutely right. I won't worry anymore."

Situations that make us nervous or uncomfortable and cir-cumstances that are heartbreaking are an inevitable part of the human experience. We must each find a way to maintain our inner peace even in the midst of these times. Otherwise worry will be the thief that steals our peace of mind and any chance of enduring happiness.

Several years ago I was at church listening to a Christmas mes-sage when a handful of words struck me deeply. They have been the focus of my reflection on many occasions ever since, because they speak to something that we all struggle with, and perhaps something that I struggle with more than most. These were the words that moved me that night: "We are afraid because we don't know *how* things are going to work out, but things *are* going to work out."

As I look back on the things I have spent endless hours worry-ing about, they never worked out the way I thought they would, but they did work out. Many years ago now, I was engaged to a wonderful young woman, but for a number of reasons it didn't work out and we broke off our engagement. I remember feeling sad and lost. It seemed like a disaster. As time has passed, it has be-come abundantly clear that we came into each other's lives for a reason, but the reason wasn't to marry each other. If we take some time to look back at the things that we have worried about, we will discover that things rarely work out the way we think they will, but they do work out.

I don't want to pretend that we do not experience problems and suffering and death, because these things are real. They are, however, a part of our experience, part of the journey, and part of the process of becoming perfectly yourself.

Worry is one of the psychological barriers that we must learn to manage if we are to experience enduring happiness. It is not one of those things that we can overcome once and for all. It is more like an addiction that must be managed one day at a time, one situation at a time, and when things get really bad, one moment at a time. Like so much of what we have discussed in this book, there are no easy answers or solutions to our wrestle with worry. This is soul work, and soul work takes time and constant effort. There are, however, some very practical steps we can take to avoid being paralyzed by worry, steps that will also promote a greater sense of inner peace and enduring happiness.

THIS IS THE PROBLEM

"Life is difficult." This is the simple observable truth that thrust M. Scott Peck onto the world stage. It is almost an understatement of the obvious once we begin to reflect on it, but by the time he wrote these words in the latter part of the twentieth century, people were drunk on the exuberance of Western peace and prosperity and had begun to think that life would or should be easy.

Problems are inevitable in a marriage, in a career or business, and in health and well-being. And yet so often we seem shocked, stunned, amazed, and generally taken by surprise when they emerge. We deceive ourselves by convincing ourselves that they won't happen to us, only to other people. The problem is not that there are problems. The problem is that we think that there shouldn't be problems. Subconsciously we often foster the expectation that life will go along without any problems. Intellectually we know that problems are inevitable, and yet we spend a lot of our lives trying to avoid problems, pretending that they don't exist, or being surprised when they make a cameo appearance in our lives.

I am not suggesting that we should go looking for problems. I would like to suggest, however, that problems have a place in our lives. They occur for reasons that sometimes are obvious at the time and reasons that sometimes take years to unfold before us and within us. How we deal with the inevitable problems of our lives can radically affect the level of happiness we experience on a daily basis. If we treat every little hiccup as a major crisis, then we are going to be constantly stressing ourselves out. For instance, I travel a lot. My staff and friends will tell you that I can be particular. I like organization and, like most people, I like what I like. But when you are traveling, you are at the mercy of so many circumstances beyond your control. So I have to sit myself down and get myself into a "go with the flow" mood; otherwise, I will allow the tiniest things to wind me up, which is exhausting and robs me of my capacity for joy.

Most things I get myself worked up about are of absolutely no consequence. I suspect the same is true for most people. In the grand scheme of things, they are irrelevant. In many cases, it is simply a matter of preference. But once I have started to wind myself up, if someone tells me that I need to relax, I get even more wound up. It irritates me. I know they are right. I know that I am torturing myself because I had some false assumption that everything would go the way I wanted it to. But as I have already mentioned, situations almost never unfold as we expect them to. It is really our expectations that torture us. Who creates these expectations? We do. We choose our expectations. We choose to drive ourselves crazy.

Every day we encounter problems. The doctor was running late, and you had to wait an hour. Your flight was canceled. Your daughter was sick, so you had to take the day off from work to look after her, but you also have a huge project to finish. Your brother and sister are in an argument and they are both trying to pull you into it. You've just ended a relationship and you are questioning your choice . . .

Everyone has different ways of responding to the problems of daily life. Some people avoid them. Others blow their problems out of all proportion. They allow themselves to become completely overwhelmed by how enormous they have imagined their problems to be. Some people look for problems. They find their identity through their problems and choose the role of the suffering victim. Whenever you meet them and ask them how they are, they always have some problem or illness that they are struggling with. Other people seem to take their problems in stride with no fanfare at all. Others simply shut down in the face of problems and become unable to function. And then there are those rare souls who seem to respond to any problem, large or small, with a calmness that puts others at ease. They are able to face their problems, assess the situation, and begin to work through them.

Problems are opportunities to build character. The problems that we encounter each day give us a chance to abandon our egos and our overindulged personal preferences in order to grow in flexibility and patience. Problems are one of the time-tested paths to personal growth. The most significant periods of growth occur for most people when they are faced with problems. In fact, many of us ignore the need to grow until we are faced with problems.

Times of peace and prosperity often make people and nations lethargic, even lazy. But when times get tough, people rise to the occasion and draw on their best selves.

It has been my experience that men and women can endure just about anything as long as they see themselves moving toward a worthy purpose. The question we must now ponder is: Do the problems of our lives have a purpose, or are they simply an error in the cosmic design and the human experience?

Every problem that occurs in our lives comes to teach us a lesson. The lessons can be understood only in relation to our essential purpose, which is to become the-best-version-of-ourselves. Every time we encounter a problem, we should ask ourselves: *What can I learn from this situation? How can this help me to become a-better-version-of-myself? What particular virtue can this problem help me to grow stronger in?*

Suffering is unavoidable. The first of Buddha's four noble truths is simply "Life is suffering." We don't need to go seeking it, because in many ways, large and small, suffering will find us. But we make sense of suffering by seeing it in relation to our purpose. An athlete endures the suffering of training by keeping his goal in sight. Suffering is the fire that refines the gold that is your character.

You cannot avoid problems and suffering, but you can avoid the lessons they have come to teach you. This is wasted suffering. It is like a man who goes to the gym and lifts weights for hours every day but does not know the proper shape and form each exercise should take. He puts in the hours, he suffers, but he is worse off than before he started because he has done damage to himself.

So add this to the short list of things you can know for certain: There are going to be problems. The nature and scope of the problems we face will vary from day to day and year to year, but every day we are going to find ourselves in situations that we don't like and that just don't turn out the way we would like them to. So now that we know problems are inevitable, we should start to prepare ourselves to respond patiently and calmly when they arrive.

The problem is not that there are problems. The problem is that we do not prepare sufficiently for the problems we know we will inevitably face. We know the storm is coming. We may not know when it will come or what it will look like, but we know it is coming. The best preparation for the storms of life is to build character one virtue at a time.

If you wish to know someone, really know someone, do not form your opinion of her by what she says and does while she lives in peace and prosperity. It is easy to be kind and patient when the wind is at your back. It is well known that circumstances do not make the person; they reveal the person. Thomas à Kempis wrote, "The time of adversity shows who is of most virtue. Occasions do not make a man frail, but they do show openly what he is."

MANAGE THE PRESENT, CREATE THE FUTURE

The lesson here is calm action. Internal unrest often adds to the external unrest that problems bring to our lives. In order to deal with problems in a way that is most beneficial, we need internal peace and calm. From that inner peace will spring calm action. Have you ever noticed that in a crisis some people are able to remain calm, assess the circumstances objectively, propose a solution, manage people, and encourage and participate in a calm and measured response? It is also worth noting that those who can do this are sometimes the people you least expect. A person you previously thought to be quiet, shy, and even socially awkward can all of a sudden appear as a confident problem-solver. The reason is that for so many years he has been developing a deep reserve of internal calm, so deep that the external unrest cannot disturb it. Interior calm gives birth to calm action.

Calm action allows us to most effectively manage the present and create the future. Interior calm and clarity are the roots of calm action. So let us explore the ways we can begin to create this interior calm.

Our lives are moving at such a relentless pace in this modern age that we very rarely stop to reflect before making decisions in our daily lives. The faster and busier our lives become, the more we rely on our conditioned responses. In deciding what to eat or drink, we often delegate this decision to an already formed habit. This is just one simple example of how we respond to certain daily situations. If something doesn't turn out as we would like, perhaps we shout at someone or slam a door, or maybe we take a deep breath and begin to calmly talk through contingency plans. Whatever our response is, it has likely been practiced a thousand times before. It isn't as if we sit down to think about what has just happened and then start shouting. The way we respond to so many situations every day is more of a reaction than it is a reasoned response.

In order to respond in ways that are healthier for us and healthier for the people around us, we have to take time to reflect before we are even in these situations. Once we are caught in the moment, we are more likely to react than to reflect. Over time as we grow increasingly aware of the length of our own fuse and how we react in a variety of scenarios, we will be able to begin to develop the ability to pause (controlling our conditioned responses), breathe deeply, assess the situation, and then respond (creating a new and more positive conditioned response). The difference between reacting and responding is that a reaction is automatic every time, whereas a response is specific to every situation.

Too often we make the mistake of thinking that the question is "What should I do?" Sometimes—more often than you would think—the question is "Should I do anything?" Sometimes the best thing to do is nothing.

In this book we have been exploring the balance between accepting ourselves for who we are and challenging ourselves to change and grow. In this context, the great challenge is to discern which parts of ourselves need to be accepted as they are and which parts need to be challenged to change. This is the same kind of balance we are looking for between knowing when to act and when to leave a situation alone. There is a prayer that speaks to this dilemma and has managed to cross denominational and religious lines to become one of the most commonly invoked of our times. It is invoked by millions of men and women around the world every day:

> God, grant me the serenity to accept the things I cannot change, courage to change the things I can, and wisdom to know the difference.

This is the balance we seek, allowing action and inaction to coexist. The balance that allows serenity, courage, and wisdom to cohabitate in our hearts and direct the actions of our lives. It is this serenity, courage, and wisdom that give birth to calm action. But all too often our hearts and lives are filled with restlessness and not serenity, fear and not courage, and ignorance and not wisdom.

Sometimes when you are reading, certain words touch you. They resonate so deeply within you that they stop you. Occasionally when I am signing books after one of my seminars, someone will come to the head of the line with a book that is well worn and well read. As I flick through the pages, I discover the phrases and paragraphs that they have underlined. I am always fascinated to see which words caught their attention.

Hardly a day goes by when I am not stopped by words on a page that peer into my own life to encourage me or challenge me, but few times have I been brought to such an abrupt halt as I was during my first reading of *Letters to a Young Poet*. In late 1902 Franz Kappus, a student and aspiring poet, wrote a letter to renowned German poet Rainier Maria Rilke. It took several weeks for the letter to reach Rilke, who was traveling and working abroad at the time, but when he received the letter, he replied at some length and in some detail to the questions that Kappus had posed. This began a great friendship of letters that lasted for more than five years. In his fourth letter, Rilke writes something to the young poet that speaks directly to our struggle to find the balance between discerning and deciding, between acting or waiting, between the now and the future:

> Be patient toward all that is unresolved in your heart and try to love the *questions themselves* like locked rooms and like books that are written in a very foreign tongue. Do not seek the answers, which cannot be given to you now because you would not be able to live them. And the point is, to live everything. *Live* the questions now. Perhaps you will then gradually, without noticing it, live along some distant day into the answer.

Oh, that we could learn to love the questions themselves. This is what our information-addicted culture has lost, a simple love of questions and mysteries.

I have a journal that I call my Dream Book. In it I write about places I would like to go, things I would like to do, books I would like to write, things I would like to own, and qualities I would like to possess. But I also write down favorite quotes or specific insights that strike me along the way. On one page I wrote this in large lettering: "Learn to enjoy uncertainty. Uncertainty is a sign that all is well. God is your friend and the Universe is your friend. Between them, they will take care of the details." This is one of the great struggles of my heart. A few years ago when I wrote this entry, I realized that I had become so used to having my days, weeks, and months planned out that in many ways I had lost my capacity to enjoy uncertainty and to act spontaneously. It was my reflection in the classroom of silence that allowed me to realize this and that has also allowed me to transform this aspect of myself and my life.

Only in the classroom of silence can we gain the calm and clarity that allow us to know when to wait patiently and when to push forward impatiently, when to plan diligently and when to live spontaneously. It is in the quiet of our own hearts that we learn how to calmly manage the present and passionately create the future. It is this calmness and clarity that will allow us to realize what we are called to and what matters most. Finding our place in the world and beginning to fulfill our mission is then nothing more than a matter of time. A man or woman who takes time in quiet reflection sincerely seeking to find his or her place in the world will not be ignored. First will come the inner calm, then will come the desire to serve, and then will come a wonderful clarity of purpose. Guided by that calm and clarity, we begin to affect what we can affect, and only then do we truly begin to *have* an effect.

Franz Kafka, Austrian poet and philosopher, expressed it in this way:

You need not leave your room. Remain sitting at your table and listen. You need not even listen, simply wait. You need not even wait, just learn to become quiet, and still, and solitary. The world will freely offer itself to you to be unmasked. It has no choice; it will roll in ecstasy at your feet.

Of all the people in my life, I hold those who taught me to be quiet, and still, and solitary in highest regard. In a number of passages throughout this book I have tried to pass their wisdom on to you where it seemed most appropriate. I do not even wish to ponder the quiet desperation that I would have experienced had they not emphasized the importance of learning to be comfortable in my own company and of befriending silence and stillness.

We cannot discover who we truly are and what we are here for—we cannot become perfectly ourselves—amid the noise and confusion of the world. As often as possible, we must step back from it all and reconnect with who we are and what we are here for in the classroom of silence. It is these times in silence, stillness, and solitude that allow us to make sense of all that is life. These are great friends to have—silence, stillness, and solitude—and they will give you the gift of calm action.

THE OPPORTUNITY CLOCK

What were they thinking when they named the alarm clock? *Alarm* suggests fright, fear, chaos, confusion, and looming catastrophe. Who wants to wake up to that every morning? I was at a dinner earlier this year with Ken Blanchard and five or six other business leaders when Ken referred to it as an opportunity clock. I liked that. Each day is brimming with opportunity, but we so often allow ourselves to become overtaken by reactive behavior. The alarm goes off, and we get up. The phone rings, and we answer it. And on and on it goes. This type of reactive living allows whoever and whatever is the loudest to take our lives hostage.

From the moment we wake up each morning, we have to take hold of our days. This is when we need to get ourselves in a "go with the flow" mood so that we don't allow the unexpected problems of the day to trip us up, but it is also when we need to set the direction and agenda for our day.

I am a better person when I enter my day slowly. We all have a reflective self and a task-oriented self. Which do you think wakes up first? The task-oriented self wants us to start rushing around doing things from the minute our feet hit the floor in the morning. Most people get so carried away by their task-oriented self that it could be midmorning, even midafternoon, before they are aware that their reflective self is alive. The task-oriented self will get the job done, but if we don't consult with the reflective self, we may very well come to the end of the day and discover we filled our day with all the wrong things. They seemed urgent, but they weren't really important.

The task-oriented self will sacrifice your workout time to answer e-mails that could have waited. The task-oriented self will skip lunch and overload on snacks in order to get a little more work done. The task-oriented self will downplay the importance of time in the classroom of silence, telling you, "You don't have time for this. You have things to do!"

You need to enter your day slowly. Get to bed a half hour earlier and get up a half hour earlier. Take some time to read and reflect. You will be amazed how this changes the focus and energy of your day. This is the way to calm action.

Every morning before I go anywhere, I have to get myself into a place of gratitude. When I am not grateful, I am pretty much at my worst. For me, my level of gratitude is a pretty good measurement of my health of mind, body, and spirit. When I am in a place of gratitude, nothing bothers me; the daily trials and inconveniences seem to just slide straight off my back. But when I lose that inner gratitude, the tiniest things drive me crazy. No. Let me restate that: When I lose that inner gratitude, *I let* the tiniest things drive me crazy. So one part of my morning rituals involves getting myself in a place of gratitude. There are times when the opportunity clock goes off and I don't want to get out of bed. That is a critical moment of the day, when we experience the first victory or the first defeat of the day. At that very moment, body and spirit are wrestling for control of the day. From time to time I will tell myself, *I will just lie here and do my gratitude exercises.* On other days when my task-oriented self gets hold of me, I tell myself, *I will do my gratitude exercises in the shower or while I am driving to the office.* These are self-deceptions. While this is happening, the inner voice is whispering, *You are always happier and you always have a better day when you take ten minutes to sit down in a quiet room and do your gratitude exercises.* But I must say there are too many days when I ignore that inner voice even though it has never led me astray.

You may be wondering what my gratitude exercises are. They are so simple. I start with my gratitude list, a list of all the people, things, and opportunities I am grateful for. What's on the list? My family, friends, health, food, clothes, my home, my car, money, meaningful work, my staff, my audiences, my office, new opportunities, dreams, faith, books, music, my talents and abilities, travel, nature, and so on. Sitting still and quiet, I begin to reflect on each of these, allowing the blessings of the past and the possibilities of the future to emerge from within me. From time to time negative thoughts will come and try to steal me away from my gratitude meditation, but when I realize this is happening, I try to return immediately to where I was on the gratitude list.

I also carry it with me in my wallet so that if I feel myself slipping into an irritable, restless, discontented mood, I can take a couple of minutes and use it to get myself back to a place of gratitude. Gratitude is really important for me. It's a touchstone. For you it may be something different, but my experience leads me to believe that when we are in a state of gratitude, everything is a little brighter.

More than ten years ago in one of my earliest works, I wrote, "Joy is the fruit of appreciation." It remains one of my most cherished lines, and I often use it to inscribe books. If we truly seek this enduring happiness, the lasting joy, that we have been speaking of, let us find a place in our daily rituals to remind ourselves of all we have to be grateful for. In gratitude, our hearts always dance for joy.

The ninth lesson for enduring happiness is this:

PATIENTLY SEEK THE GOOD IN EVERYONE AND EVERYTHING.

Some people seem more naturally disposed to looking for goodness than others, and again, I have to admit that I am not one of them. One aspect of my work is to observe people and society and to assess what is not working in people's lives and in our culture. The danger here is that I can get into the habit of overlooking what is good and wonderful. Each day, I have to remind myself that despite the suffering and heartache we inflict on ourselves and on others, life is amazing and this truly is a wonderful world.

Patiently seeking the good isn't always that easy, especially when things don't go how we would like them to or when people hurt us deeply. And yet for all its hiccups and heartaches, life is worth living and we generally find what we are looking for. Those who believe people are basically good seem to be happier than those who believe that they are not. Those who believe that good things are going to happen to them are generally happier than those who do not. And what's more, good things tend to happen to people who believe good things are going to happen to them.

The problem with patiently seeking the good in everything and in everyone is that you won't always find it. It is one thing to have a buoyant spirit, but it something entirely different to ignore the fact that there is evil in our world.

There are events that appear to be complete manifestations of hatred and evil. These situations are often diabolical and devoid of good. We shouldn't pretend otherwise. When evil visits our lives or the lives of the people we love and care about, there is no benefit to anyone in the mistaken notion that it has happened for a good reason. Good things may come from these horrible situations, but that will only be because good people will restore hope and love to the lives of those who have been harmed by evil. We should avoid the temptation to sugarcoat the reality of evil when we come face-to-face with it. Fortunately most of us very rarely, if ever, face a situation of this magnitude.

But in our overly judgmental and hyperanalytical culture, we are often too quick to point out the negative in situations and people. The ninth lesson encourages us to slow down a little and celebrate the good in everyone and everything.

One of the very practical ways we can live the ninth

lesson occurs whenever we find ourselves in a situation where ideas, opinions, and expectations clash. Next time you are in an argument or a disagreement with someone, try to identify three things you agree on before you begin to voice your disagreement. When you voice your disagreement, begin by talking about what you have in common with the person you are arguing with. Too often we rush to judgment, race to argue, and overlook all the common ground we share. I see it in businesses and in churches; I see it in schools and in politics. If we engage the ninth lesson for enduring happiness and patiently seek the good in everyone and everything, we will begin to celebrate our common ground more and more. This common ground will be the territory that we expand as we grow to understand each other's perspectives and points of views in new and dynamic ways. We agree on much more than we disagree on, and yet we rush to disagreement.

Let us begin today to develop the habit of seeking the good in everyone and everything. That doesn't mean you will always find it. From time to time, you will be disappointed. But we should strive to make this our first inclination, our default position. In most cases I think we find what we are looking for. The other option is riddled with problems both personal and interpersonal. If we don't go seeking the good, then we will be constantly looking for what is wrong in everyone and everything. This attitude breeds dis-ease, a discontentment and unrest within that sooner or later manifests itself in our lives, whether as a health problem, the breakdown of a relationship, or dissatisfaction at work. Sooner or later, everything within us seeks an external expression.

Is it easy to foster this attitude of looking for the good?

No. But it is possible. Let us not seek what is easy. Let us boldly seek what is possible. And over time and with practice, every good habit becomes easier to exercise. Ralph Waldo Emerson wrote, "That which we persist in doing becomes easier—not that the nature of the task has changed, but our ability to do has increased." This truth can be applied to each of the nine lessons.

Patiently seek the good in everything and in everyone. The more you seek it, the more you will find it. The more you find it, the more you will emulate it. The more you emulate it, the more you will inspire others to reach out and grasp all that is good, true, noble, and beautiful in this life and in each other.

Applying the Ninth Lesson for
Enduring Happiness:

PATIENTLY SEEK THE GOOD IN EVERYONE AND EVERYTHING

I will apply the ninth lesson for enduring happiness
to my life by taking the following steps:

1. I will be mindful of the time and energy I direct toward worry. When I realize that I am worrying or fixated with a situation, I will try to step back from it and calmly ask myself these questions: Is there anything I can do about this situation? What lesson can I draw from this situation? If I can take some positive action, I will do so immediately. If the situation is entirely out of my control, I will try to surrender to whatever virtue can be gained by it.

2. Each morning I will establish a "go with the flow" attitude within myself and nurture it through the various situations that arise throughout the day. Mindful that things rarely turn out as I expect them to, I will not approach situations with rigid expectations but rather with a healthy curiosity about the outcome. Uncertainty is my friend.

3. I will grasp the first victory of each day by getting out of bed at the very moment the opportunity clock goes off. Once up and ready for my day, I will pause to reflect on the day before me and to remind myself about what matters most. I will resist the temptation to let my task-oriented self rush me into today's activities prematurely. I will connect with my reflective self by moving into my day slowly.

4. I will look for the good in everyone and everything. As I move through my days, I will proactively seek the good in people and in situations. When I find good, I will celebrate it by complimenting people and expressing my appreciation. From time to time, I will pause to reflect on all the good that is within me and all the good things I have done in and with my life. There are times to reflect on the ways we can improve, but I will remind myself that this is not one of these times. I will devote this time exclusively to celebrating the goodness that is within me and to the ways I have shared that goodness with others and the world.

Home

I love the feeling of coming home. Each year I spend about two hundred days on the road, so I get to experience the feeling often. Whether I have been gone for a couple of days or a couple of weeks, there is something wonderful about coming home to your own sacred space. There is nothing like the feeling of coming home.

Growing up in Australia, I never imagined that I would live anywhere else, but having lived here in America for several years, this is where my life is now—this is home. It is always incredible to see the harbor with the bridge, the Opera House, and the cityscape as I fly into Sydney when I visit family and friends back in Australia. I love them and I love being there, but after a couple of weeks I start to itch to get back to my life here in America.

Happiness is feeling at home with ourselves, with who we are and where we are and what we are doing. It is that warm, comfortable feeling of familiar surroundings and the acceptance of good friends. I suspect that if we can foster that feeling of being at home within ourselves, the rest is just details.

I was in Los Angeles recently, listening to the closing comments at a conference I had spoken at, when a handful of words struck me as words do only very occasionally. In her closing comments the conference organizer quoted these words of poet and lecturer David Whyte: "Anything or anyone that does not bring you alive is too small for you." How I wish I could embrace these simple words with every ounce of my being, and having embraced them and celebrated them in my heart, how I wish I could live them in every moment, giving my time and my energy only to the people and passions and things that bring me life, and turning my back on the things that bring any kind of death to me, however small.

Let this idea guide you. Whatever is stopping you from becoming the-best-version-of-yourself, cast it from your life . . . and whatever is helping you to become the-best-version-of-yourself, embrace it with all your heart, mind, body, and soul. If you are to be happy, it will be as yourself—not as what someone else wants you to be or expects you to be or wishes you were but as your own wonderful self.

Whether you received *Perfectly Yourself* as a gift, borrowed it from a friend, or purchased it yourself, we're glad you read it. We think you will agree that Matthew Kelly is a most refreshing voice, and we hope you will share this book and his thoughts with your family and friends.

If you are interested in writing to the author, wish to receive his free newsletter, *The Beacon*, would like information about his speaking engagements, or would like him to speak at an event you are hosting, please address all correspondence to:

The Matthew Kelly Foundation
2330 Kemper Lane
Cincinnati, OH 45206
Phone: 1-513-221-7700
Fax: 1-513-221-7710
e-mail: info@matthewkelly.org
www.matthewkelly.org

MATTHEW KELLY is an internationally acclaimed speaker and author. His books have sold more than one million copies and have appeared on dozens of bestseller lists including: *The New York Times, The Wall Street Journal, USA Today,* and *Publishers Weekly.* Kelly's titles include *The Rhythm of Life* and *The Seven Levels of Intimacy.*

During the past decade more than three million people in fifty countries have attended his presentations and seminars. He has given over 2,500 keynote presentations for a variety of organizations including Fortune 500 companies, national trade associations, universities, churches, and non-profits.

Kelly is the president of Beresford Consulting, Inc., a consulting firm focused on teambuilding. He is also the founder of The Matthew Kelly Foundation, a non-profit whose primary charitable focus is helping young people to discover their mission in life.